We're All Rubber Bands

Finding happiness with who you are

By Robyn Thorn

This book would not have been written without the unending support and love from the following:

My dad & Mommala

My sister and brother-in-law, Audrey & John

My brother, Jason

My amazing Honey Bees

My Dining Divas

My Little Sister

All of my Zumba Peeps

My "sisters" and "family" out there who have my heart

My karaoke krew and fellow band geeks

and finally,

The best extended family a girl could ever ask for!

Several years ago, I was up late getting my place ready for my niece to come for a weekend visit. I moved from one room to the next, making sure everything was fresh and clean and ready for her to arrive. My mind began wandering, as the tasks didn't really require any deep thought. It was then that it hit me.

I'm a rubber band!

Sure, that's a strange thing to think, but bear with me as I attempt to explain this statement. During our lives, we all have our ups and downs. We have moments when we feel like our feet aren't even touching the ground because something amazing has happened. Other times we find ourselves on the opposite end of the spectrum, and it takes every ounce of strength just to get out of bed in the morning.

What I observed that night in my own personality is that, regardless of how thin I'm stretched emotionally, I always snap back to who I am naturally. I believe that person to be an optimist. I look for the good in others or in a situation. I hope for the best outcome for me or for a friend or loved one. I know that everyone has their struggles and it may be my encouraging words that come at just the right time to prevent their band from snapping.

As I mentioned, deep down I've always been an optimist, but I, like you, have had my share of heartbreak and struggles. You will understand what I mean with the very first chapter, which is the reason I first started writing. We each have our own battles that can be hidden well, and I was a master at that.

What has helped me in going through the process of writing this book was letting go of what has happened to me and finding the happiness in living my life and celebrating the successes I've experienced along the way. I am both figuratively and literally finding time to stop and smell the roses…and jasmine…and honeysuckle.

In the chapters ahead, you will walk with me through times in my life that I hope you will identify with in some part of yours. At the end of each section, I will compare how I feel now versus how I felt then. Many of these emotions were incredibly raw at the time they were written, but fortunately, time gives us perspective.

I have learned much over the years and continue to do so every day. I don't expect everyone to always lean towards optimism, but rather I hope that as you progress through this book, you will find comfort knowing that the pendulum will always swing the other way. It's that balance that brings us back to our center.

Here's wishing you discover your rubber band as well. If yours was stretched too thin too many times and its ends have frayed, then I implore you to tie them together and look at it in a new light. Consider it a battle wound. Consider it a reminder of harder times. Consider it proof that you're stronger than you thought you could be. Other parts of your band may feel weak, but not that knot. *That* part represents a lesson that didn't defeat you. It allowed you to realize that regardless of the number of knots in your band, it is the knots that make you whole.

I think it's a pretty safe assumption that most everyone has been in a situation where someone says something to you or asks you a question that throws you off guard, and it isn't until later that you come up with a witty comeback. For example, I was walking through the mall the other day and one of the ladies working at a kiosk in the middle of the mall walked up and said, "Can I ask you a question?" to which I quickly replied, "Sorry, I'm in a hurry." As I walked away I realized I should have said, "You just did. Thanks!"

Sure, this usually happens every once in a while to most people, but imagine being asked this type of question every time you meet someone new or someone you haven't seen in a while. Imagine wanting to make a smartass remark but knowing that it would only unnecessarily hurt the person's feelings for what seems like such a benign question.

This has been my dilemma for 10+ years now. Anyone who has met me knows pretty quickly that I'm married and have two dogs. The question that is almost *always* asked is, "So, do you have kids?" It's just like a knife through my heart every time I hear it.

For those of you who don't know, my husband and I have been battling fertility issues during our marriage. We've been married for over 14 years now but have only been on the doctor path for the last 10 of them. During this time, I've taken fertility drugs – oral and injectable, had so many ultrasounds I could be an ultrasound tech, doubled as a pin cushion because of all the bloodwork that's been done on me, had surgery, and even gone through two fresh in vitro fertilization rounds as well as two frozen ones with the last fresh cycle resulting in a miscarriage…all with nothing to show for it except heartache after heartache. This really only slightly touches on everything I personally have been through.

So, imagine then, failing at something you want so badly only to have it thrown back in your face every time you meet someone new or someone you haven't seen in a long time. One thing you learn how to do is put on that happy face and resist the urge to hurt the person who unknowingly hurt you by asking that question. Again, it's a completely benign question this person has asked. Benign or not, it doesn't make the reality any less painful. Feelings have to get buried…deep. It's a defense mechanism that I've gotten very good at over the years.

For most people, getting pregnant isn't something they thought much about…it just happened like it's supposed to. Please know that I am very happy for anyone who *wants* to get pregnant and can do so easily, as this is not something I want to have in common with anyone. Try putting yourself in the place of someone who has struggled with this for years and years. There are constant reminders *everywhere*! Hell, you wouldn't be here if it weren't for your parents being able to reproduce. Because you spend so many years putting on that happy face for everyone, many people don't know just how much it hurts…especially hearing someone say, "You want my kids? I'll sell them to you for cheap!" Again…resisting the urge to bitch slap that person takes every ounce of strength in me!!

One of my favorite insulting comments is, "My sister/cousin/friend/neighbor adopted a child and then got pregnant!" Ummm…last I checked, adoption wasn't a fertility treatment. Don't get me wrong, I'm very happy for them, but there are no guarantees of having a biological child of your own after adopting.

Many of you may be wondering how I feel about adoption. I am utterly and completely open to adoption…always have been. There are so many children out there who deserve to know what real unconditional love is and who may have never experienced it. I know I have so much to give. So then, your next question must be, "Well then, why haven't you adopted yet?" My answer...*sigh*...is that this decision can be a difficult one to convince other people to agree to when they don't want to give up hope or would be happy to just do without.

Right now, even the thought of getting pregnant scares the hell out of me because I, more than most people, know that just because the test results are positive doesn't mean that everything will work out. I have cried with several friends and family in the last few years for this very reason. The pain is unbearable and can be only lessened slightly with time...at least in my experience.

What I'm learning now is that at some point, feeling more like in the very near future, the dam *will* break, and not only is it scary to think of what will flow out when that happens, but who will get caught in the floodwaters. I've felt lately like the little Dutch boy who is quickly running out of fingers to plug all the holes in the dam I've built over the years. These overwhelming feelings affect every part of your life, every relationship you have, and can even cause you to doubt everything you know and once believed your life to be. Every journey must have an end...I'm just having trouble seeing the light at the end of my journey as nothing more than a train headed right for me.

So, my dear friends and family, my hope with this is that you will be more aware of your blessings. You may not have had to work hard for your child(ren), if you've been so blessed, but please be aware that this doesn't come easily for others. Everyone has their battles; some are more difficult than others. Some battles affect them only for moments, while others have an enduring effect on every relationship and part of their life. They make us who we are as does every other struggle we go through. As I continue to deal with this, I know that the dam may break, but I hope I've made it to high enough ground when it happens to be able to point out the dangers to others below.

This issue consumed my life for a very long time, but I finally feel at peace with it all. I would love to say that we were finally able to achieve pregnancy, but, as we all know, many stories don't have a happy ending. In the end, we realized that we had differing opinions on adoption and amicably decided to end our marriage. I have never and will never blame him for how he felt, as that is a very personal choice. He is a good person, and I genuinely wish him a happy life. He definitely deserves it.

As for me, I still struggle with the never-ending questions and comments. There are times it gets to me, but I don't dwell on it anymore. If motherhood happens, it happens. If it doesn't, I'll continue to be just fine. Being happy with who I am is much more important to me. I don't think this makes me selfish, as it's been a long healing process. It's something I felt I had to mourn, but just like losing a loved one, it can still sneak up on me from time to time. That's okay when it happens. Most people will never know what I went through or how difficult it was. I wouldn't wish it on anyone. What I find amazing is that the happy face you see me wearing now isn't hiding anything. I am happy.

Tee hee hee!

I could never be an actress. There, I said it. Sure, I love movies and can quote a large number of those in my collection, but there is one reason why this would **never** be my profession. Once I hear something that makes me laugh, it takes me FOREVER to stop giggling. I have a feeling I'd be replaced by a frustrated director on take 427 because I'm doubled over hysterically laughing at the stupidest thing. I know I get this from my family. I've lost track of how many times we've sat around the dinner table listening to my dad try to tell a joke only to get tickled at the punch line that only *he* knew. It would usually get to the point that watching him try to compose himself was way funnier than the joke turned out to be.

Just the other night I was telling a friend something I read online. When I got to the part where I was finally going to reveal the part that cracked me up, I started laughing. I could NOT get the words out. I actually had to type what I was trying to say, but even then I could barely open my eyes to see the keyboard. I think you could have blindfolded me with dental floss!

Today I had to stop off at Time Warner Cable to drop off some equipment I didn't need anymore. I took my number, and while I waited, I decided to peruse Facebook. I came across a short video of a cat and thought I'd check it out. Since I had my Bluetooth in, I figured no one would hear. I'm not sure what was so funny about it, but it cracked me up. Now, I know we all have experienced the act of trying to refrain from laughing at the wrong time or place.

Some examples of this would be a business meeting, a yoga class (been there, done that!!), at your place of worship, or...in my case...waiting for my turn at my local cable company office in a lobby FULL of people. I tried thinking of something serious or picturing the looks I'd get, but that made it worse. I am proud to say that I was able

7

to pull myself together and make it through my turn, but that was a test of self-control right there!

After getting home this evening, I was texting with a friend when his phone decided to interject with its own version of what it though he needed to say instead. It turns out his phone is a bit racist!! I am SO GLAD I wasn't drinking anything at the time, because my TV across the room would have been covered in whatever it was.

Life gets way too serious sometimes. We often forget it's meant to be enjoyed. I think that little interludes of laughter can do so much good in one's life. I'm sure this will trigger some funny memories for most, but at a minimum I hope you find that for just a few minutes your face remembers just how good a smile feels.

Sometimes I just need a good laugh. The stress melts away and my cheeks hurt from smiling. I believe that a sense of humor is something to be valued, and being able to laugh at yourself is even more amazing. I always find joy in making others laugh and believe wholeheartedly that a smile goes a long way. Despite all the struggles I have gone through and will go through in my life, it honestly amazes me that I can still see the humor through the darkness, the laughter through the tears, and the smile on the faces of those whose lives have touched mine.

Finding Comfort in a Blinker

I had a quiet ride home tonight as I watched the wipers clear the raindrops from my windshield. I followed my normal route, occasionally changing lanes when necessary. I guess I'm one of the rare drivers who actually uses their blinker. As I listened to the steady metronome, I found it brought me back to my childhood. Most people wouldn't think a simple turn signal would do that, and I'll admit that it surprised me as well.

When I was a young girl, I would often ride in the back seat of my parents' car (or station wagon, depending on how far back we go) heading towards home late in the evening. I would be drifting in and out of sleep as my dad made sure we got home safely. I can remember sitting there with my eyes closed listening to the sound of the road and the occasional noise from the blinker. I used to play a game where I'd try to see if I could figure out where I was based on the direction we turned. Every so often I'd fall asleep, but there was something I really enjoyed about the quiet drive with my family that gave me a sense of security, knowing I was in good hands.

Most of the time while driving now, I can be found doing my best impression of what the game show "Dancing in the Car" would look like. I assure you…I'd win that one every time! Plus, someone has to entertain the masses on the ridiculous commute we must endure each day. Sometimes, though, after a rough day of impersonating a sponge at work, I'll drive in silence on my commute home just listening to the steady sounds that accompany my movement across the lanes of traffic. Who knew you could find comfort in a blinker?

I have so many wonderful memories of my childhood, and this is still one of them. It seems like such a simple recollection, but so many people I know haven't been as fortunate as I was in the fact that I have an absolutely amazing family. I continue finding comfort in a blinker, but every day, I find comfort in knowing how lucky I am that a simple blinker can cause me to count my blessings.

Life has a funny way of being the ultimate teacher. It can impart wisdom in the least expected places. With this in mind, I pass along the following in an effort to pay it forward:

1. It really is okay to break the rules every once in a while. It can even be a lot of fun!
2. Life is a marathon. If you treat it as a sprint, you might injure yourself and miss out on something important.
3. The easiest way to learn something new is to jump in with both feet, but the easiest way to learn something new about yourself is to mess up BIG!
4. You can transform yourself, but be careful that you don't forget about the inside transformation while you concentrate on the changes on the outside. These can sneak up on you.
5. It's amazing how something as simple as a genuine smile can instantly put a person at ease.
6. It is possible to learn to run…and enjoy it…even when you aren't being chased.
7. It's better to regret the things you have done than those you haven't.
8. Old habits may die hard, but they can also come back from the dead to bite you in the ass!
9. It is possible to watch a movie once, hate it completely, and then laugh your ass off at it every time it comes on TV.
10. Angels show up when you least expect them, but evil is usually in disguise and is really good at impersonations.
11. Sometimes it's important to be a lot more action and a whole lot less talk.
12. It's never too late to straighten your teeth…and it's definitely a lesson in patience.
13. Guilt is not an emotion I'm a fan of, but it's one of the strongest ones out there because it can serve as a conscience

when you've lost yours.

14. Starting something new can benefit more people than just you.

These last ones I learned from my dogs, Maggie, Button, & Max:

15. Don't bite the hand that feeds you. Kisses are much more effective.
16. A dog wearing a cone can be both the saddest and funniest thing at the same time!
17. It is possible to teach an old dog new tricks.
18. It is necessary every once in a while to assert your dominance.
19. A stranger is a friend you haven't met yet.
20. Love is unconditional, forgiveness is universal, and whatever someone wants to call you is okay as long as they call you with love.

From those who have walked alongside me through these lessons to those from whom I've been taught a lesson…THANK YOU!

The thing about learning is that you have to be open to it. When you are, the possibilities are endless!

I'm a firm believer that sometimes a message is put in front of you at just the right time, allowing you to truly receive it the way it was intended. Earlier today, I saw an image that said, "Never waste your time trying to explain who you are to people who are committed to misunderstanding you." That struck a chord with me, as it helped bring closure to something I had been struggling with for a while. I'll admit that things like this happen fairly often in my world, so I've learned to be open to those messages when they appear before me.

We *all* deal with struggles of our own. I know I do. More often than not, those around me are unaware of the depth of what I'm dealing with, as I do so privately. I've learned that all I can be is who I am, and people will either accept me or they won't. After all, have you ever tried to convince someone that you're not crazy without sounding crazy? Yeah…good luck with that one! If I were you, I'd refer to the above quote for help with that situation.

The last two years have been quite an adjustment for me. I'm getting more comfortable with everything, but every so often something sneaks up on me. It's times like this that a friend will say something to me that makes all the difference. What was interesting today was the very same quote that had such a profound impact on me seemed relevant to a friend of mine who was dealing with some personal issues of her own. Since it helped me so much, I decided to pay it forward. The conversation went like this:

Friend (after reading the quote I sent to her):
"Oh wow, thank you!! You are such a true and genuine friend and person."

Me:
"Thanks! Means more than you could possibly imagine."

13

Friend:
"You're definitely a gem in this crazy and cruel world."

Me:
"Ditto doll!! Us gems have to stick together and make sure no one takes away our sparkle!!"

Like I said, sometimes you just hear exactly what you need to hear at just the right time. Today was proof that, along with chocolate, friends are the best invention ever!!

Friends may come and go, and words, though brief at times, can leave a long-standing mark despite your best efforts. I truly believe that compassion and empathy are two very important qualities to possess, but on occasion, someone may not hear your message the way it was intended. They may not see past the happy-faced mask they wear, and this can distort everything in their view. You can't always control how your words are received, but you <u>can</u> choose to speak from the heart with kindness and love. Doing so is the only way to keep your sparkle's luster from dulling.

A while back, I was sitting at dinner here in Austin with my mom and some friends I grew up with back in Ohio. We all sat around visiting while we waited for our food, and the kids played on various iPhones and iPads. I turned to their mom and said, "Watch. I'm gonna freak out Bryce." He was the oldest of the kids. I got his attention and watched as he paused his game. I then told him that when his mom and I were his age, there was no such thing as a cell phone or home computer and the internet didn't exist. I watched as his eyes grew big and he exclaimed, "HOW DID YOU SURVIVE?!?!"

We all had a good laugh, but he made a good point that kids today will never understand. In the last decade or so, we have grown accustomed to being able to reach someone at any moment. There's rarely a time when I receive a phone call without knowing beforehand who is on the other end. If I need the answer to a question, I can just pull up a browser on my phone as opposed to thumbing through the pages of a *World Book Encyclopedia*. We have become so connected to each other that we have begun to disconnect from those sitting right next to us.

I was recently watching *Star Trek Into Darkness* and started laughing when I realized that their communicators are basically cell phones with the speakerphone always turned on. Back when the original series came out, this type of technology was AMAZING! Now, I watch this wondering how they don't have a better means of communication in the 23rd century. Even Uhura was wearing a "futuristic" Bluetooth device as a part of her signature look. I remember as a kid watching *The Jetsons* and thought how cool it would be to talk to someone over the phone and be able to see them at the same time…enter Skype!

The truth is, as a child I survived just fine not having these advances in technology. Would I go back to the way it was? Well, of course not, as the conveniences of today are extremely enticing, but there is something to be said for being able to disconnect and live in the moment. I know I'm guilty of having my head buried in my phone while I'm out, but that's usually when I'm alone. After all, there was a time when I would be away from home and be COMPLETELY unreachable. It didn't mean I was lying in a ditch by the side of the road, but rather it was just the norm.

Considering the technology that surrounds us today, I wonder what kinds of things I can bring up that would freak out a kid born in the decades to come. Maybe it'll be something like the fact that we drove our cars on the GROUND or that our houses weren't self-cleaning. Now that I think about it, could someone work on that last one?!?! We need that invention PRONTO!!

This is something I think about quite often. I am never the first to buy a new gadget, but I'm fascinated by the things people have come up with as each year passes. There are things today that we use on a regular basis that we can't imagine our lives without, yet many of us have done just that. I do my best to put my phone away when I'm spending time with someone, as I usually want to be in the moment. I've often joked that cell phone cameras are simply a way of reminiscing about something that just happened.

After all, I worked at a drug store growing up and sold 35mm film...yes, FILM! You actually had to take all the pictures, drop them off to get developed, and then...wait. Yep! There was no instant gratification. The closest you came was either a Polaroid or 1-hour photo development. Things like this make me wonder what will become the norm in the next five, ten, or even twenty years!

Driving Me Mad

Every time I watch the beginning of the movie *Office Space*, I feel the frustration that Samir experiences as he's sitting in his car stuck in traffic hell. I also know too well the look of annoyance on Peter's face as he moves from his stagnant lane to the fast-moving one only to have them switch roles just as he arrives in line. I'll admit I've used my share of swear words when, for example, I'm stuck behind and next to cars that are both going the same speed and I can't get around either. It's at times like that that I wish I could flash a sign to them asking if ONE OF THEM would speed the **enter expletive here** up!! As I was driving back from Arlington this weekend, I too experienced many of the same emotions, and it got me thinking about something I refer to as *car*ma and traffic math.

I'm sure we've all witnessed carma. Typically, it only happens to *other* drivers. For example, there's the person who you'd been stuck behind for miles only to finally get around them. They then try to not only pass you, but the cars in front of you as well. The problem is, they're now stuck behind a big 18-wheeler and apparently no one else wants to let them in. Gotta love teamwork!

Now, traffic math is something that's always baffled me. You don't typically see this in smaller towns, but it is definitely alive and well in the Austin area. Thanks to the magic of GPS, we can now find out how many miles it is to get from point A to point B. Let's say our destination should take 20 minutes to get there. When you factor in traffic math, that length of time can be shorter or longer despite taking the same route. Variables that affect traffic include time of day, day of the week, and other drivers who have somehow avoided the pitfalls of carma...so far. What would normally take 20 minutes could end up taking double that time or more in some cases.

I have also found that there are several things that other drivers

17

can't quite get the hang of despite the rules being very simple. First on the list are stop signs. For some reason these confuse many people. Often, you'll come across those who don't feel the rules or etiquette apply to them, while others apparently need an invitation to go on their appropriate "turn."

Secondly, the concept of merging is something that is baffling to many drivers. I think of it as shuffling a deck of cards. As one card from the left stack falls, it is followed by a card from the right. This process continues until all the cards have been used. Seems simple, right?!

Finally, when in traffic, it is best to keep a safe distance from the car in front of you in case they come to a quick stop. Now…FOR THE LOVE OF ALL THAT IS HOLY, that distance does not have to be equivalent to four football fields!!! These drivers are the reason traffic exists in the first place. After all, traffic wouldn't occur if the person in the front would just move!!

I will admit when in a hurry, I tend to be more like Samir while driving. I always talk out loud to the cars around me, expressing my frustration at the predicament in which I've been placed. When on a long road trip, however, I tend to provide entertainment for those around me. It is at these times you can find me both singing and dancing in my car as I continue with the stop-and-go traffic, knowing that I will *eventually* arrive at my destination.

I'm still hoping for the day that either flying cars or teleporters are invented. It looks like science has their work cut out for them. I guess in the meantime, I'll just deal with constant and never-ending road construction, traffic math, and the invention of new and colorful metaphors to call those around me as I drive to point B.

Over the last few years, I've learned a few tricks when it comes to a long commute. I've become a fan of podcasts and have started many a conversation with the phrase, "So I was listening to this podcast on the way here, and **enter interesting fact or story here**." I wish I could say I experience extended moments of Zen while driving, but sadly I'd say my temperament is closer to Yosemite Sam on a bad day. I do find that music can calm the savage beast and still enjoy entertaining others with my seated dance parties. After all...sometimes you've just gotta dance it out!

Tests

The vast majority of the population gets nervous at the thought of having to take and pass a test. There's usually a lot riding on the outcome of your effort. The tests we're most familiar with as we grow up are due to a class in school or college and may even be taken using one of those super cool Scantron answer sheets so you can find out quickly just how badly you did. What I have found interesting in my life thus far are not the tests where the results end in a number, but when they end in a lesson that challenges you both morally and emotionally.

I think of these tests, we'll call them Life Tests, that I've had in the past; some I've passed and some I've failed *miserably!* Regardless of the outcome, as I look back on them, I realized that with each one I learned something about myself, the situation, or another person. Now normal tests, like those in school, were always *following* a lesson. I guess they work that way so you know which kind it is.

Identifying the type has never been the problem for me. I was always a good student and was probably harder on myself than my parents were. I graduated high school with honors, got a college degree, and even earned my teaching certificate. I still enjoy learning about all types of subjects, from astronomy to Greek mythology to history.

I get a kick out of learning something new as this "mouth of unwanted knowledge" is always looking for more interesting facts to fill up this sponge of a brain of mine. What fascinates me is when I don't realize I'm in the middle of a Life Test until it's too late. It's like those recurring themed dreams I have where I'm in school or college and I have a test or performance that I haven't prepared for and I'm just expected to "go with the flow," so to say. Those are not very restful nights.

So what happens when a Life Test comes up that rocks you to your core and all you can wonder is "What the hell am I supposed to learn from THIS mess?" We all know that hindsight is always 20/20, but when you're in the middle of the exam, you can't exactly look around at other people's Scantron forms for the answer. It's always something you have to figure out for yourself, and sometimes that answer doesn't come as easily as you would hope. It makes you wish you had a cheat sheet for every Life Test out there that included some secret formula that you could plug the variables into and it would spit out the answer. Of course, the constant in all of my formulas is me!!...therein lies the problem!

My dad used to tell me that a person could solve their problems by just amputating from the neck down. My problems always come about from the part that's left over...my brain. I tend to overthink *everything* in my life. I ask, "Why am I feeling this way?" or "Should I be feeling this way?" or "What got me feeling this way?" It's a constant battle between my brain knowing what the right answer is and my eyes and heart seeing it in time to avoid the repercussions of having to use the CliffsNotes instead.

Maybe friends, family, and therapists should really be considered your study partners during these Life Tests. You bounce ideas off of them and they in turn bounce ideas back, making you see the lesson through fresh eyes. That new perspective allows you to realize that each time you face something unfamiliar, you have to reinvent the wheel by coming up with a whole new formula specially made for this situation. I can only hope this constant personal development reveals someone who is stronger, both physically and emotionally, and even more prepared for those times when I haven't had a chance for a late-night cram session.

You'd think as you grow older that these Life Tests would lessen. The joke with that is that they do, but the risk you take by giving wrong

21

answers goes up. Each test seems to come with higher stakes despite the fact that they may be fewer and further between. The great thing about these later-in-life tests is that your cheat sheet consists of the sum of all your experiences up to that point and what lessons you actually learned from them.

Sometimes I Stop and Wonder

Spend any time with a child and you'll find yourself being asked the craziest questions. I love the utter fascination they have with everything they experience. It's always captivated me how a kid's mind works, but I'm also finding that my brain can give them a run for their money from time to time. Every so often, random thoughts pop into my head, and I often wonder if others have similar moments.

Tonight, while peeling a kiwi, I was thinking back to the avocado I had earlier today and thought, "It sure would be weird if all foods of the same color tasted the same." Seriously though, what if an orange and a carrot tasted alike?...or a steak and a piece of chocolate?...or a blueberry and...ummm...something else blue. Now that I think about it, there aren't a lot of naturally occurring blue foods out there.

That thought reminds me of a question I was once asked on a job application. It said, "If blue was a breakfast food, how would it taste?" Yeah...ummmm...let me ponder that for a bit. As I just mentioned, there aren't a lot of naturally blue foods, so you gotta love a question with no "right" answer.

I guess that defines life, really. There are no right or wrong answers, just decisions to be made. You're presented with two choices. Whichever decision you make determines the path your life will take.

I find it sad though that as we get older, we lose the outlook on life that we had as kids. Just tonight I watched a video of a little girl named Kayden who was experiencing rain for the first time. The utter joy she showed is something that is rarely seen in an adult. Don't get me wrong, I don't expect to see an adult standing outside in the rain squealing in delight unless you're in an area that is in a severe drought.

What I mean is that we often take things for granted as an adult. We don't stop to smell the flowers or even look more closely at them to appreciate how complex they really are. We worry too much about our first-world problems like when you don't realize the time changed on your cable TV guide and you spend several minutes looking at shows that just ended. This afternoon, instead of listening to the TV, I got to listen to the sound of rain and thunder outside. It was something I hadn't heard in a while, and I found myself stopping to appreciate the comforting sounds. I wonder how many people did the same thing.

I hope I always retain my sense of wonder mixed with twisted humor. It definitely makes for a more entertaining world. So many people I know seem to have lost that part of them. To be able to see the world through a child's eyes is quite a gift.

We learn to stop taking things for granted. We find the wonder and beauty in the simplest things. We are able to laugh at something mundane. We learn the most important lessons that we have forgotten as we've aged.

I recently watched a video of a little girl who was given a beautifully wrapped box. It was a present from her mother. When the little girl opened the box, she lit up upon seeing what was inside. It wasn't a new phone or game or even a doll. It was a paperclip. That's it – a paperclip. To this little girl it was the most amazing gift ever, and the joy she felt was obvious. It melted my heart! THAT is the joy and wonder with which I hope to view the world as each year passes.

Transforming Fear

So many times, I've decided not to do something I wanted to deep down simply out of fear. Sure, I'm afraid of heights and quite claustrophobic; however, the fear to which I'm referring doesn't necessarily have to do with me getting hurt physically, but rather emotionally. I'll admit that on occasion my fear is justified and it poses as my emotional bodyguard. On the other hand, there are times that it's just an irrational annoyance that's trying to keep me from having a little fun or experiencing something truly amazing.

Over the last few years I've basically been flying by the seat of my pants when it comes to the direction my life will take. I will be the first to admit that I may not always make the right decision or even the smartest one, but I find when I make a decision by setting fear aside, I rarely have regrets. Sure, I may get hurt in the end, but I *always* learn something from the experience. I guess this new mantra of overcoming my fear will turn out to be the transformation I need.

I recently heard someone say that you regret the things you didn't do more than those you did. I would have to agree with this wholeheartedly. Living with the wonder of what would have happened is far more crippling to me than doing something a little risqué and not liking the outcome. I don't owe anyone an explanation for why I choose to do the things I do. That is my business. It may sound harsh, but I don't want to live a life of "what ifs."

Let's be honest...my idea of doing something a little crazy may be closer to what some people consider boring. Oftentimes, I'm reminded of something my dear friend once told me. She said that personal growth doesn't occur unless you step outside your comfort zone. To me, that was a bit of a challenge and has helped me move forward in my personal development. I guess from time to time it's okay to give my emotional bodyguard a night off.

I forgot! It's not like me to forget, but nonetheless I did. I forgot how good it feels to take care of me for a change. I guess life sometimes gets in the way, and it takes a moment of clarity to serve as a catalyst. I've done it many times before. I've had that amazing feeling that comes from knowing you're doing something to better yourself. Lately those times have been few and very far between. I've been trying to figure out why it's been put on the back burner, and it made me think of the time I just needed a flip.

If you've ever been to Texas during the summer, you know it can get miserably hot. Now I know that we're right in the middle of a love affair between Old Man Winter and a very confused Mother Nature, but bear with me—I swear I'm going somewhere with this. Getting into your car during the summer months is brutal, and if you've ever felt the hot metal from a seat belt burning your flesh, you know what I mean.

Because of this, many of us have chosen to purchase those nifty doodle sun visors to help reduce the amount of sweltering heat our vehicles can produce…that is unless you're one of those crazy people who likes to bake cookies on the dash of your car. (Yes, people really do that here!!) I too am one of those who jumped on the visor bandwagon in an attempt to save myself from third-degree burns in July.

Now, of course I didn't get one of those accordion visors or even one that folds neatly. Nope! I inherited mine from my amazing parents, and it's one that you have to know how to twist just right in order to collapse it into a little a space about a quarter of its original size. After what felt like months of faking that twisting process, usually with my tongue sticking out to help aid in the process, I finally figured it out.

My problem then was I couldn't figure out why the stupid things kept falling down when I'd put them in the window. I'd try resting one on the other. I tried wedging them behind the rearview mirror. I even tried balancing each visor just right so it would serve at least the majority of its purpose. Of course, I'd usually just curse them when they fell, say, "SCREW IT," and get out of the car, knowing it was going to be ridiculously hot no matter what I did.

It wasn't until one day, while being blinded by the sun, that a light bulb went off in my head. The answer to this frustrating problem was a simple flip. You see, each visor wasn't a square, it turned out that it was a rectangle. You almost can't tell as the edges are rounded. Apparently, I had been trying to balance them on the long side which was making them too short to be held in place. Once the flip occurred, I could hear the angelic chorus singing, "Hallelujah!!" It worked!! Now, I'm sure it *may* have made my car a few degrees cooler (if any), but at least I had solved the mystery of the great visor debacle. All that trouble and the answer was a simple flip.

Just like my visor conundrum, my life can use a flip every so often. When the flip occurs, I find it usually makes a world of difference. So far, I'm enjoying the new outlook. Here's hoping you find your flip!!

I can easily get into a rut between work and various "adulting" activities. Many times, it feels as if things will never change when all of a sudden that flip happens again. It could come in the form of an "AHA!" moment or just simply a change of scenery that awakens your inner gymnast. The flip happens, and my dull routine is turned on its head in a good way. Sometimes it comes in the form of an attitude adjustment or the realization that I've been taking certain things for granted. Either way, the flip changes my perspective, and it's just what was needed.

So often we lose sight of what's important. We get caught up in unnecessary drama or we focus on the negative and forget just how fortunate we are. I'm grateful for every day I can wake up, walk on my own two feet through my apartment in which I can afford to live, and prepare for the day ahead…even if it means I'm going to practice the fine art of holding down the couch.

I never know who will get in touch with me during the day, but I've found many times their call or text or email comes at just the right time. In my case, it can mean a visit from a dearly departed friend through a dream that brightens my day. It can be the advice from a sibling that helps point me in a new direction that I never would have headed towards otherwise. It could be the person who answers the phone with a contagious smile in their voice that snaps me out of my trance.

You see, it is one another that makes the emptiness bearable. We are social creatures. I was recently watching a movie with a very dear friend. In the movie, the main character was a young man who decided to give up all the luxuries we've grown so accustomed to and travel alone. What he witnesses is stunningly beautiful. It was then my dear friend stated that all those experiences are bittersweet because he has no one to share them with. It was as if his journey was the fallen tree in the forest. It made a sound, but there was no one around to hear it.

It is now a new year, and with a new year comes a new beginning. We all know our time here is borrowed. It is what we do with our time that matters. I can't speak for anyone else, but I intend to make the most of my time while I've still got the time.

The months and years seem to pass by more and more quickly.

We seem to be in a hurry in an attempt to get everything done. What I still feel is important is taking the time to be present in our lives. Take in the beautiful sunset. Listen to the words of a friend without thinking about what you will say next. Embrace a loved one and let them be the first to pull away for once. Put away your phone and just unplug. Time will pass no matter what we do, so make the most of what time you've been given.

What is nothing? Is it the absence of something? Some people think nothing would just be blackness, but that, by definition, is something. I'm not sure my brain can really grasp the concept of nothing. We've lived our lives learning names for everything. I read recently that they just discovered a new part of the body located in the knee. Before it was discovered, was it nothing? I'm sure the person who injured theirs didn't think so.

So, what do we do when our minds get so jumbled up that we would give anything to turn it off and think of nothing? I know this has happened to me many times. I've talked with a multitude of friends who have dealt with this same affliction. It's as if we just want the world to stop for a few minutes...or hours...or days, and let our minds rest. Some people find that just sleeping is enough, but if you've known me for any amount of time, you've probably heard me tell a crazy story about a dream I've had and how detailed they can be. That goes to show that my mind won't even shut up when I'm asleep!

What I've learned is that it is not always what I'm thinking that I need to change but rather what I'm doing at the time. Sometimes just relaxing with a good friend, swirling a glass of wine and talking is enough to calm the waters. We all need to remember that life is meant to be enjoyed. I'm not saying it's going to be "sunshine and roses" all the time, but it could be as simple as taking the time to appreciate the sunshine and roses that have gone unnoticed that would make all the difference.

Not being able to turn off my brain is exactly what got me writing in the first place. I found that once I put down on paper or in a blog what I was thinking, I could finally decompress. Clearing my mind is easier said than done, so finding an outlet that works can make all the difference. To this day, writing still helps. It allows me to focus what, at first, appears to be nothing, but turns out to be the very thing keeping me awake at night. I've always liked organizing things, so it makes sense that organizing my thoughts brings me peace.

It's amazing how much of our lives we spend waiting. We wait in lines at the airport, in the waiting room at the doctor's office, or on a weekend trip stuck in traffic. I'm sure if we add up all the hours, it would come to a staggering amount of time wasted. So, if they say that good things come to those who wait, then I'm thinking that right about now most people should be expecting some pretty good things headed their way. I would like to think I'm one of them.

About a month ago I badly rolled my ankle playing a game with a football and have had my patience tested as it heals. I have been unable to teach my Zumba classes, which is something that I love doing. I have been forced to slow down and become more sedentary, which is not something I enjoy. I want nothing more than to go for a run or go out dancing, but instead I sit at home with my foot up as I let it rest. I've at least confirmed with an MRI that nothing was broken or torn, but nevertheless, the healing process is a very slow, very tedious progression that gives me no choice in the matter.

In today's world, we always seem to be in a hurry. We have cell phones that give us more power in our hand than the Apollo spacecrafts had onboard on their missions to the moon. We have microwaves that heat up our food or drinks in mere seconds compared to how it was done when I was a kid. We no longer have to wait for a letter to arrive in the mail thanks to technological advances. They've even built toll roads that allow us to drive much faster speed limits so we can cut down our commute time.

Now, I'm not saying that *everything* in our lives is faster and better, but when something that is normally fast (by today's standards) slows down, or rather slows *us* down, we become instantly impatient. Imagine the last time you pulled up a website and it didn't load immediately. Did you sit there patiently? Nope, you probably yelled at the screen or had a few choice words for your internet provider. The last time you were stuck in traffic, did you hope and pray that someone wasn't seriously injured, or did you wonder why things like this always happen to you when you're running late?

This week I had lunch with a dear friend who reminded me of something. She mentioned that she was learning to be thankful for what she has and is spending less time asking for things to go her way. I've been thinking about that today. When I hurt my foot, I could have very easily broken or torn something that required surgery, but did not. I have a roof over my head and am able to pay my bills thanks to a job I enjoy. I have wonderful friends and family who would drop anything to help me out.

I'll admit that I get too caught up in the rat race from time to time, but I have *always* been the kind of person to stop and smell the flowers, both literally and figuratively. Am I going through some sort of test at this point? I'd probably say yes, but fortunately for me, I was always a good test taker.

It is said that someone has to learn patience, and I'm a good example of that. I'm constantly learning. I'm constantly being tested. I fail at it quite often despite being a good test taker. For me, having to be patient for whatever reason is always an opportunity for some inner reflection. In the grand scheme of things, does that extra minute I was delayed make or break the bank? No. Remembering that is what will afford me a passing grade when my patience is being tested.

A few years ago, I was at home and something amazing happened. I can't remember what it was, but my first reaction was to call my mom and tell her. As I was approaching the end of the story, my mom stopped me and said that I had already told her about this. I interjected and said that it had *just* happened, and she was the first person I had told. Her response should really be put onto a shirt. She said to me, "Oh. It's amazing how quickly we forget the things we didn't already know!" I'll give you a moment to take that one in and chew on it for a bit.

I processed what she said for a few moments myself and then knew I HAD to write that one down!! My parents are full of gems like that. I never know what they'll say next. Pondering this memory tonight got me thinking not about all the things I know, but rather about all the things I've forgotten over the years.

I've always been the kind of person who remembers my dreams. I don't just recall bits and pieces of them, but every single detail about them. It always fascinates me when I wake up from such a crazy or scary or emotional dream that I think will change me forever only to forget the whole thing by the time I've finished drying my hair. Considering how often I remember my dreams, I've probably forgotten thousands of them over my lifetime. That's crazy to think about.

Speaking of drying my hair...I can't tell you how many times an idea for a blog has popped into my head, and I almost write the entire blog with my head flipped upside down. I tell myself that this brilliant idea will still be there when I have time to sit down and write...and then...yep! GONE! The harder I try to remember them, the deeper into my subconscious my ideas sink until there's no sign of them anywhere.

I finally wised up and started jotting down the ideas on my phone so I'd at least have a starting place when I do find I have some free time. The only bad thing about this is that I find the inspiration doesn't flow like it did when the idea first popped into my upside-down head. There's no telling how many thought-provoking blog posts have been lost into my neural quicksand.

So now I wonder what other things I've forgotten. I KNOW that I no longer know much of what I learned in school and in college. Once the test was done, that information was GONE! I'm sure I've also forgotten many people over the years who I felt were important at the time. Now, they're not even a distant memory. Will I continue to forget things? Sure, but I just hope that the important things stick. Unfortunately, where I park my car on a daily basis is a memory made of Teflon.

When I really think about it, the sheer amount of information I've forgotten must be astounding! Maybe that's why I find the brain so fascinating. I'm sure every experience I've ever had is stored somewhere in the deep abyss of my memory, but I just have no access to it whenever I want or need it. Until we get to the point that we can bring that to the surface, I'll have to use the collective memories of all those with whom I come into contact to piece together the parts of my past that remain out of my mental reach.

Life doesn't get easier, you just get stronger. The pendulum of life swings both ways. Sometimes everything is coming up roses while other times you seriously think the damn thing has you stuck in some sort of sick *Groundhog Day*-type of situation. The problem is you never know when it's gonna swing the other way, and you have no way to know for how long it will remain headed in that direction.

While we all enjoy the ride when things are going our way, it is when the opposite occurs that our true character is exposed. Do we handle the challenges with grace or do we fall down on the floor and throw a temper tantrum?

The other day I saw a video a friend posted on Facebook of the newest addition to his backyard pond: a turtle. The turtle was determined to escape from the rock-enclosed surroundings by slowly climbing up the sides. Several times you see it roll back down to the bottom only to try to make its way back out again. There is no telling how many attempts this poor creature made only to have its efforts foiled again and again.

As I was watching the video, I started my own narration based on what I figured the poor little thing was thinking. Some of the time I figured it sounded like Yosemite Sam as it bounced back down the sides looking like the large plastic disc in the "Plinko" game from *The Price Is Right*. Other times he just acted like he wasn't surprised and was just enjoying the spinning scenery during the tumble back down. I guess we all tend to respond to situations like our friend the turtle. Sometimes we're mad as hell and other times we just go with the flow.

Just knowing that the pendulum is swinging is what keeps us sane. After all, it can't be bad ALL the time...right?! Maybe it's not that something is necessarily a negative, but rather that we've developed new coping skills to help us through the tough times. We are constantly evolving and learning from past experiences, which in turn changes our perspective.

Maybe like the turtle, we've climbed up enough rocky enclosures only to find ourselves right back where we started. Again and again we brush ourselves off and grow wiser with each attempt. We've learned the important rule: That which does not kill us makes us stronger. Sure, we may end up on our shell every once in a while, but if you don't stick your neck out, you'll always feel like you're stuck between a rock and a hard place.

I read something recently that struck a chord with me, and I found it very profound but funny at the same time. It said, "When you trip on one step, you don't just throw yourself down the stairs." We all do this from time to time. I mean, who hasn't cheated on a diet once or twice? So you got off track. It happens.

Throwing a virtual temper tantrum because you messed up isn't going to solve anything. Stop. Breathe. Regroup. Strength comes from realizing that we are imperfect creatures and we WILL mess up occasionally. Try to remember that learning from our missteps is what makes the trips worthwhile.

Lesson or Blessing

"We met for a reason. Either you're a blessing or a lesson." I recall having a conversation with a very dear friend about the fact that when you meet someone, it's either for a reason, a season, or a lifetime. I think that's true as well, but lately I've found that most of the people I meet turn out to be either a blessing or a lesson. The frustrating part is that this determination cannot be made upon meeting someone but rather after the fact.

I go into a relationship or encounter with a new friend optimistically, but it's only later when I look back with eyes wide open that I am able to see things clearly. Sometimes my optimism is validated, while other times I find myself reeling from an unexpected heartache. I do believe that I learn something from both experiences, but I will admit it is usually the negative that sinks in faster and has more staying power.

Letting my guard down is getting more and more difficult lately as I seem to be meeting more lessons than blessings. Being able to count on someone is very important to me. Being able to trust what they say as the truth is paramount. When their true personality is revealed to be less than honorable, it causes that emotional barrier to slowly inch its way back up. This causes an internal struggle, as I am typically a very open and positive person.

Does this mean that with every person I meet, I'm going to go through this potential turmoil again and again? That's a very high possibility, but I refuse to let them win by turning me into a pessimist. I will take the lesson I've learned from that experience and move forward. I will wipe away the tears and step up to the plate again, hoping for something other than a swing and a miss. This will be *my* way of turning even the hardest lesson into a blessing in disguise.

This has rung true over and over again. I wouldn't say I have a permanent barrier up, but I find it easier to sift through the bullshit than I did years ago. I will always let my guard down for the right person, as I have always been one to wear my heart on my sleeve. What I'm discovering is that I am actually learning from the lessons of my past. I am becoming wiser. I am finding my voice and speaking it loud and clear when I feel I am receiving less than I deserve. That, in and of itself, is very empowering.

This doesn't necessarily refer to dating, but to any relationship. So many times I found myself hurt by someone but never spoke up. How could I expect things to change if I didn't say anything? Again, speaking with love is all I can do. Those who truly care will be open to hearing what I have to say. Those who don't...well, those are the blessings in disguise, and those relationships have a way of working themselves out.

The Lost Ark

Every so often we find ourselves in the "ebb" part of the ebb and flow of life. It's almost as if Murphy himself is testing out his law on your life and one thing after another makes you feel like you're Sisyphus watching the boulder roll down the hill just as you got it up to the top. It's during times like that which makes me say, "Please stop the ride! I wanna get off!!" When I hear that a friend is going through a difficult time like this, I usually remind them that the pendulum will eventually swing in the other direction and offer an ear or a shoulder.

What many of us forget is just how powerful that ear or shoulder can be. I'm not saying that we've miraculously developed some sort of superhero power…although that might be exactly what we've done without realizing it. Instead of a cape, we are seen as wearing a halo of sorts. So many times, our words or actions have arrived at exactly the right moment for the person to whom they're directed. It may be just what that person needed to hear or could be as simple as the embrace of a hug after a difficult day.

As each of us has our issues we deal with, we must recognize that everyone else is also fighting their hidden battles. Most people will put on their happy face and show you what they want you to see. On days like this, a simple smile or even a two-second text can go a long way; it can make all the difference. It can pull someone up from the end of their rope. It can instantly change their attitude by making the unbearable downright tolerable. You may not even realize you've done anything to merit gratitude, but that's what makes such a simple act so powerful.

Late last year I took a trip back up to Arlington to visit my family. On my way, I did something I've NEVER done. I purchased a pack of cigarettes. Now, before you start lecturing me about the dangers of smoking, let me qualify this statement and put your mind at ease. I

40

did NOT purchase the cigarettes for myself, nor did I pay for the entire pack myself.

I had stopped at a convenience store for a drink or a snack or something and found myself standing behind a young woman in line. She was there to purchase a pack of smokes but was having trouble coming up with all of the cash she needed and was told she was about $0.22 short. She told the cashier she would be right back and stepped outside to her car to see if she could scrounge up the missing money. I stepped up to the counter to pay for my item and asked the clerk how much she was missing. When he told me the amount, I took a quarter out of my wallet, tossed it on the counter with the rest of her change, finished paying for my stuff, and then headed out the door, passing by the young woman as she was headed back in looking completely discouraged.

As I got all of my stuff situated in my car and started to back out, I looked up only to see the young woman frantically waving at me with an ear-to-ear grin. She was thanking me for my help. I really didn't think a quarter would have made such a difference, but to *her* it did.

The point is that we all have our vices. Sure, hers may have been cigarettes, but I am not one to judge. Hell, I could have been buying some chocolate treats that I needed like I needed a hole in the head for all I know. She may have just had the worst day ever and all she wanted was a drag of a cigarette to make it a little easier. The bottom line is that her reason doesn't matter. The look on her face before the quarter and after the quarter said it all. I had made a difference in her life on that day and, although I would never condone smoking, I will admit her reaction made the rest of my drive that much better.

Now, I usually don't do this, but I'd like to pose a challenge to all of my readers. Your mission, should you choose to accept it, is to commit as many <u>A</u>cts of <u>R</u>andom <u>K</u>indness during the month as you can. See how many people's lives you can have a positive impact on in one month. Smiles are contagious as is laughter, so I challenge you to find a reason to smile and laugh every day and see how many people you can infect with a positive attitude.

Make that call to a long-lost friend or relative you've been putting off for one reason or another. Look for joy in the little things and share that view with those around you. Compassion for others is a lost art nowadays, but the great thing about life is that it becomes what you make of it. Remember, your life is an occasion. Rise to it!

A smile really does go a long way. For some, however, finding their smile can be difficult. I still find that by helping others with their struggles, it helps me put mine in perspective. I truly believe that, if we all took time out of our lives every so often to lift others up, the world would be a better place.

Focus

Last July I was lucky enough to have LASIK surgery. I'm happy to report that everything has healed as it should, and I'm enjoying being without contacts or glasses for the first time since 7th grade. Prior to the surgery, I was very nearsighted. It wasn't until something was about 6" from my face that I would see things clearly. Now, I sit here at Starbucks on a beautiful Sunday afternoon and I can read everything around here with no effort. Having focus is good, but it's not always easy to come by.

Life gets busy; it gets complicated. Losing focus is something that happens and can be difficult to get back. Years ago, when I would go see a movie, it always drove me nuts when they would start the reel and it would take a minute or two of everyone in the theater crossing their eyes before they would finally focus the screen. If only it was that easy. Life pulls you in a thousand directions and prioritizing can be a challenge.

So how do you find your focus once you've lost it? Some people just push through it while others find themselves feeling completely defeated. One person might retreat and internalize everything when another will reach out to friends and family for help and advice. My point is that losing focus affects everyone differently. Remember you're a unique person…just like everyone else. What works for one person isn't going to work for the next. The good thing is that there is no right or wrong way to get back on track. It's all trial and error.

Lately it's felt like it's been a bit of a struggle for me. It's been a huge adjustment over the last 11 months, but I have a good foundation for what's to come. I have a great job in a place with people who I feel truly care for my well-being and who want me to be successful. I have an amazingly fun second job where I get to help people achieve their fitness goals while acting like a goofball as I dance around on a

43

stage wearing a microphone. I have the unending support of my family and friends, who mean more to me than I could *ever* express. I **know** it just takes that one moment for something to happen that will snap me out of this blurry stage of my life and I will find the wind at my back helping me along.

In the meantime, I will count my blessings. I will learn something new. I will set goals. I will appreciate dancing in the rain. I will *try* to remember that it is ALWAYS easier to give advice than it is to take it. Most importantly, I will allow myself the time I need to finally adjust to the idea that things don't have to be figured out all at once.

Every part of my life doesn't have to be in focus at the same time. It will eventually all come together. Just like my eyes after my LASIK surgery, I need to allow myself time to heal. For a while now I've been making things up as I go along, and it can be exhausting at times. I'm not sure what is in store, but this I do know: it is much easier to fly by the seat of your pants when you're not battling a headwind!

I waited a very long time for things to truly come into focus in my life. Someone said something to me that struck a chord, and since then, I've been trying to live by that mantra. She said, "Don't prioritize your schedule. Schedule your priorities." Talk about the flip I needed!!

Making this book a priority and scheduling time to work on it was a perfect example of this. I'm sure many of us can think of a million things we should prioritize, but how many people remember themselves in the process? When you put everything else first, you miss the most important lesson: nothing works if you don't.

So much has happened over the last few months. For those of you who didn't already know, my marriage of 16 years ended on September 6th. I am newly single. I am living alone for the first time in my life. I am trying to find a full-time job. I am adjusting to everything I have known for most of my adult life being changed all at once. I know that I am NOT the first person to go through this, and I unfortunately won't be the last, either. I am also not the first person to get rejected at interview after interview...although it feels like that right about now. There are so many things that could have caused me to just give up, but I won't let that happen. Why? Because I am Firebird!

This last weekend I had the rare opportunity to visit with a long-time friend of my brother who I haven't seen in years. That in itself is not rare, but it just so happened that the reason for the visit involved a movie that is now in theaters, and we were all there to support him. The movie is called *Unconditional,* and our friend Brent McCorkle not only wrote and directed it, but he also wrote some of the music for the movie as well.

Going to see this movie was a first for me. Not only was it the first movie that I had seen where I actually knew someone involved in a movie's making, but it was the very first time I had gone to a movie by myself...all alone...solo. I treated myself to some popcorn and a drink and went in and sat down.

There were several previews prior to the start of the movie, and I found myself a bit overcome with emotion. I knew that, based on the previews for Unconditional, that I expected it might require some tissues (and it did), but I didn't expect the reality of my situation to bring me to tears prior to the movie starting. I did my best to compose myself, and the movie soon began.

I was fascinated watching each scene because of the fact that I actually knew the writer/director. I tried to think about what he must think when watching a screening of one of his films, and I soon found myself listening for the reactions of the other moviegoers. Were they laughing at the right spots? Did they seem as engaged as I was? At one point I even realized all I could hear over the sound of my own sniffles were the sniffles of those around me. The movie was very touching and is a great example of why it is so important not to judge a book by its cover. It is one I plan to buy for sure and may even go back and see it again.

Part of the way through the movie I came upon a shocking moment. Let me first take you back with me to a day some years ago when I was looking up at a stormy sky in the middle of the afternoon. I remember thinking how ominous the sky looked and thought how dark and dreary everything was at the time. The clouds cast a shadow on all I could see and there wasn't any sign of the weather letting up anytime soon. It was then that a thought popped into my head which could only come to someone who has flown in a plane.

If you've ever taken off in a rainstorm, you know just how turbulent things can become as you ascend through the clouds. What amazed me was that once you broke through the storm, there was nothing but blue skies above you. This is something I have thought about for many years.

So now, there I am sitting watching a movie, and I hear this exact lesson being told back to me by one of the main characters in a story about an oriole named Firebird who had to learn this lesson for himself. It moved me to tears…again. This wasn't even a sad part in the movie, but there I was sitting with tears streaming down my face.

I realized at that moment that my life had been shrouded in storm clouds. It was now up to me to remember that, regardless of how turbulent my life may seem, there are always blue skies above me. It was as if I was being reminded of that fact through this wonderfully amazing movie I was watching. It was almost poetic that I was watching the movie alone, as it is alone that I again must realize this truth.

So, here I sit in my apartment contemplating the path my life is going to take. This is not the life I had planned. I'm in uncharted territory right now. I'm making things up as I go along. I'm realizing over and over that you never realize how strong you CAN be until you HAVE to be. I know it's just a matter of time before my life will have some normalcy, so I'm trying to be patient and let it play out the way it's supposed to go.

There are so many people dealing with so many more difficult things in their lives than I am, so I'm focusing on the things I am thankful for in mine. I am grateful for my health. I am grateful for my family and their health. I am so very fortunate to have the family and friends I do, as their support has been unending. I know that not everyone who goes through a divorce comes out of it thinking of blue skies. Maybe I'm a rare breed. Maybe I am Firebird. Sure, I have my moments when all I want to do is cry, but I also know that without the rain, we will never truly appreciate the sunshine.

You would never expect going to a movie to be such a profound moment in one's life, but looking back, for me, this was. It was the moment I realized just how different my life was about to become. I remember taking comfort that my tears were hidden by the darkness. I'm happy to say that I've since gone to many more movies alone. It's fun, actually. I get to sit where I want and can have whatever treat I want without having to share. Sometimes doing something solely for yourself is a nice change.

Innocence Lost

I recently changed my Facebook profile pic to one of me when I was just a wee Robyn. It wasn't just because I couldn't think of another pic to use at the time; I did so for a very specific reason. I even found myself looking at the picture for a few minutes…just staring. I saw features from both my mom and my dad. I saw my stupid cowlick on the right side of my head that still drives me nuts to this day. What I really noticed, however, was the look of wonder and innocence in my eyes.

When I was little, things were so simple. I went to school. I came home. I played with my friends. My parents provided food, shelter, clothes, and anything else I needed, including affection. I didn't always get what I wanted, but I usually got over things fairly easy. My biggest battles then probably had to do with bedtime, fighting with my brother and/or sister, and not liking what was put on my plate.

I remember thinking that I could not WAIT until I was grown up. I guess it's a good thing that back then things went in one ear and out the other, because if I had actually listened I would have been TERRIFIED of living life as an adult! What's that saying about being careful what you ask for?!

I would have heard stories about bills and grown-up responsibilities. I would have understood then that people die, relationships end, and life is full of disappointments. Some of these experiences can be so big that they can change your life forever. I would have had trouble comprehending all that I would have to endure over my lifetime. Sure, I'm being the "glass is half empty" girl right now, but it's not the easy things you learn lessons from and which help you grow as an individual, but rather it's the difficult and the trying times in which you do.

I can't tell you how many times I've expressed how much I wish I could learn something the "easy" way for once. I guess looking back, my life is one lesson after another. I wonder who I would be today had I not ignored the warnings of my elders. Who would I be today had I not made the mistakes I've made or learned the lessons placed before me?

Lately I've been wishing I could go back to that time of innocence when everything was simple. I would enjoy the theory that ignorance really is bliss and just revel in my life which lacked any adult responsibilities. I wouldn't want to have to live my life over again. After all, I think we would all agree that it is hard enough just going through your life once. I would just want to go back to that time almost as if I was on a vacation from reality. I wouldn't have to worry about doing laundry. I wouldn't have to worry about fixing dinner. I wouldn't have to worry about what is to come, because at that age, the simplicity of life would be all I would know.

Sadly, that is but a dream. The thing with reality is that it is real. Sometimes you roll with it as if you're just following the flow of traffic on the highway. Sometimes it feels like you're driving the wrong way on a one-way street. Then there are the times that it feels like your car is stuck on the train tracks and all you can do is sit and wait for the collision. I'm not sure which vehicle I'm in right now, but I have a feeling another lesson is around the next corner…assuming that's not the sound of a train whistle I hear.

I think it's perfectly normal to want to retreat to a simpler time. So often we look to our past for answers. Maybe it's our way of escaping the complications of adulthood or just pondering a happier time. After all, there are many more obstacles to overcome the older you get. Instead of finding sanctuary in our past, we need to find the simplicity in our current lives. Just like we sometimes overthink things, we can often overcomplicate them as well. I'm not saying we

49

should forget our childhood, but you can't change what has happened, only what will happen. Now is the time to make your life what you've always wanted. That's the beauty of being an adult. You can do what YOU want.

Learning to Laugh at Yourself

The other day I was teaching a Zumba class and, as I often do, I found myself giggling. If you've been in my class even once, you'll notice that I do this quite often. I love what I do, and I usually can't help but smile. For those who don't know what it is, Zumba is a Latin-based dance fitness. We do everything from salsa to bachata to reggaetón to samba and so on. It's the most fun you can have with your clothes on! It's never really felt like exercise to me, which is why I've been able to stick with it.

Whenever I talk to someone who is having difficulty with the routines, I am always taken back to the first time my cousin tried to show me how to play Guitar Hero. He made it look so easy. When I finally tried, I realized I could either strum the guitar or push the buttons, but not both!

After buying the game Rock Band a few years later, I am happy to report that not only could I play that guitar, but I've even successfully played songs on the hard level. Like with most things in life, it may not start off easy, but with practice, you can learn to overcome your shortcomings…and maybe even look a bit cooler in the process.

During one class, I happened to look over to my right and saw one of the ladies in my class bent over, laughing at herself hysterically. I instantly started giggling with her even though I had no idea what was so funny. She told me after the class ended that because of the move I was doing at that point that she realized she could do either the feet part or the hands, but she COULD NOT do them together. She was laughing at herself and found her lack of coordination at that moment completely hilarious! She was obviously having a good time, and it definitely put a smile on my face as I was teaching.

I thoroughly enjoy watching everyone doing their thing…however they wanna do it. Many times I'm giggling with someone in my class, but never at someone, as in the case I just mentioned. You see, Zumba can be a bit challenging to the coordination part of your brain. Believe it or not, even I have instances where I can't get my feet and brain to agree on what it is I'm supposed to be doing. This even happens to me during class…ask anyone!!

So…what do I do when that happens? I giggle and usually make an announcement as I correct myself that apparently my brain isn't working today. The best part of this is that it makes those who are feeling a bit less coordinated at the moment like they aren't the only ones. Zumba isn't about doing everything perfectly. It's about moving your body, having fun, and should you burn some calories in the process, so be it!

After completing my certification, a good friend of mine and my first Zumba instructor warned me of something I should prepare myself for if I was going to teach. "You will soon lose all sense of left and right." Yeah…whatever!! Ummm…she was RIGHT (or was that left) on the money! The reason for this is that when I teach a class, I am normally facing them. This means that they mirror everything I am doing.

The challenging part with this is that this now means that my right is my left and my left is my right. This is the case until I decide to turn around to face the mirror to teach a song and have now reversed everything. Now my left is my left and my right is my right. Problem with this is that most of the time I tell the class to go right I'm actually wrong. This is when the giggling comes in. What an awesome job I have where I can constantly laugh at myself and have people laughing with me!

Life is meant to be enjoyed, people! Learn to laugh when something is funny. Learn to smile when you witness something that warms your heart. Show some teeth, even!

As my cousin-in-law says, showing teeth means you're totally committed to the smile! We all get so wrapped up in our lives that we forget to see the joy around us. Try not to take some things so seriously. Remember, no one gets out alive.

Learning to laugh at yourself is such a powerful achievement. I'm happy to say I've totally mastered that skill.

You can please some of the people all of the time and all of the people some of the time, but you can't please all of the people all of the time. This is quickly becoming my new mantra. As humans, I believe we seek out approval by others. We want others to like us; we almost thirst for it at times. We want to know that what we do or say is taken in the context of how it was meant.

Approval comes in many forms – a good grade on a paper you've written, meeting someone for the first time knowing you made just the right impression, or even getting that raise you've felt you've deserved for a while. I can't imagine what celebrities must go through as they are constantly criticized by peers or, more often, by those they have never met. In many cases, their very careers depend on others liking them. If they don't have a big enough following, they'll see the success of their music/movie/team/etc. fade and, in many cases, their livelihood as well.

So often we look for approval in others when we really need to be looking inward. We need to be concerned more with whether or not we are performing to the best of *our* abilities and not worry how others perceive us.

In high school and college, I was in the colorguard. We were members of the marching band who spun flags or rifles or whatever was called for during that particular show. One of the things I always loved to do, but rarely got to, was an exchange.

This meant that you would toss your flag to someone who, at the same time, was tossing their flag to you. This always made the guard nervous until one of my instructors pointed out something that seemed so simple. If you do what you are supposed to do, then you shouldn't have to worry about catching the other flag. By this, she meant if each

54

person makes sure that their flag is tossed at the right time and in the right manner, then the flag they are receiving should be right where they expect. All of this was dependent on the occasional gust of wind, but you get the point. Once we individually did what we were supposed to do, the guard as a whole was able to complete the exchange with very few issues and, in some cases, fears.

I recently read something that made me not only laugh, but realize that it fits so many I know, including myself, to a tee. It said, "I'm a people pleaser. Is that okay?" I have tried so hard to please all of the people all the time that I forgot to be happy with my own accomplishments.

As a Zumba instructor, I am exposed to this every time I teach. Not everyone will like me. Not everyone will like my music selection or choreography. What I have to remember to ask myself is that at the end of the day, did I do my best? If I can honestly answer that question with a resounding "Yes!" then I have all the approval I need. I will also find that when I'm able to answer that question in the affirmative that the "some of the people all of the time" and the "all of the people some of the time" groups are content, and, to me, that is just dandy!!

In any position you hold, you will always face some sort of criticism. It's how you react to it that determines your success. Will I still want everyone to like me? Yes! Is that a realistic goal to have? Well, of course not! Am I working on changing that way of thinking? You bet your sweet bippies I am! Learning it's all about what I focus on at the time can make all the difference in how I feel about myself and my performance. Am I only thinking of those negative comments or do I see it as CONSTRUCTIVE rather than just criticism and use it to my advantage? Just remember, whether you are a "glass is half full" kind of person or have a "glass is half empty" type of outlook, *YOU* are the one holding the glass!

Trying to be everything to everyone is exhausting! Seriously, stop doing that. You will NEVER succeed. Being genuine and kind will speak volumes to those with whom you interact. After all, they may not remember what you said or did, but how you made them feel is what will resonate in their memory.

A Good Place to Start

I remember when I was a little kid and someone told me that they were in their twenties I thought, "WOW!! You're OLD!!" Now, being in my mid-30s, I have a completely different perspective on what is actually considered "old," let alone "OLD!!" With each birthday I celebrate, I realize that the higher the qualification for "old" becomes. I find myself looking into the eyes of an elder trying to imagine what they have seen throughout their lifetime.

This week I held my friend's eight-month-old son and began to wonder what lies in store for him. How will his experiences differ from mine? Is there any way to prevent him from going through some of the heartaches I have faced?

As I write this, I am pondering what *my* future holds. Will history repeat itself? Will I make some of the same mistakes over and over or will I finally learn from them? What important people in my life have I yet to meet? Of the people currently in my life, who am I meant to know only for a reason…a season…a lifetime? Questions like these have been playing over in my head for a while now, but with recent events, I find that they have been brought more to the forefront.

Today I spent some time with Mike, a childhood friend. It's been quite a while since we last saw each other, but just his name brings back memories. We both attended the same school from about 3rd grade until we graduated. I can recall in 6th grade, after breaking up with my first boyfriend, getting home and hearing the phone ring. When I answered it, I found myself talking to either Mike or his buddy…I can't remember who called first. Anyway, each of the boys was calling for the *other* one to see if I would "go with" (go steady with) the boy not on the phone. Sadly, I turned them both down. While sitting with Mike today, I brought up this memory of mine and it put a smile on his face. After all, that was around 25 years ago!!

57

It warmed my heart to get to share this memory I have of the two of us with him after all these years. It meant even more to me that he smiled after hearing it because he is currently at home on hospice care just a short walk from my parents' house and is now unable to speak. I shared with him and his mom what has been going on in my life. Mike lay in bed and gave us the occasional "thumbs up" which made his mom and I both smile. He yawned a few times and I'd see a tear stream down his face as they usually do when I'm tired. Each time this happened, I gently wiped the tear away with my hand. Looking back, I know this tender moment will remain in my heart forever.

After a little while longer, I could see his fatigue setting in and knew it was time to end my visit. I kissed him on the forehead and told him that I'll be back to see him next weekend. I hugged his mom and saw my way out so she wouldn't have to leave his side.

As I walked back to my childhood home, I said a prayer for him. I was so very grateful that I was able to spend some time together after all these years...I just wished it wasn't under these circumstances. I will never understand why these things happen. After all, I don't consider myself old...from my standards...and here I find myself visiting with someone who is *my age* and whose struggles I will *never* be able to fully understand.

A few hours later, my parents, my brother and I went out for a late dinner to celebrate my dad's upcoming 70th birthday on Monday. There was no cake, no singing, and no party hats, but rather the four of us sitting around a table enjoying each other's company.

We all joke that my dad is so old that he has the recipe for dirt, but even though I know he will soon be 70, I don't consider him old by any means. I felt so grateful that we could all be together at this milestone in my dad's life. Of course, it would have been better had the rest of my immediate family been there to join us, but nonetheless, we took pleasure in the fact that we were all eating a meal together. It brought me back to my earlier visit and I realized just how precious this occasion was.

I've found that the older I get, the more appreciative I am of the family and friends I have…even with all our quirks. Seeing Mike today has made that even more apparent. I would like to think that more good times than bad lay ahead, but that's the optimist in me talking. There is no way to know what is in store for me or anyone else for that matter, but however things work out in the end, I've decided that love will *always* be a good place to start.

This memory is still vivid in my mind all these years later. Sadly, the next time I saw Mike was at his funeral. It was very surreal to be there. Again, this was a childhood friend who was always kind and to whom I had to say goodbye. I will always cherish the fact that I had those moments with him and his mom. Looking back, that was a very difficult year, as I lost a total of five loved ones as well as my dog, Maggie. Each one who passed touched my life in one way or another. What I've learned from this kind of loss is that, in the end, all you're left with is love. That's a pretty amazing thing.

Lost in Thoughts

I've been sitting here for the last two hours trying to find just the right song for a Zumba warm-up and have made no progress. Everything I hear has either already been done or just isn't what I'm looking for. I find myself distracted by the smallest things like the clicking of the ceiling fan, or more pressing matters like remembering to drive to Belton tomorrow to pick up the part for the washing machine that broke tonight.

I'm lost in thought, forgetting all about the song I've been looking for, when I look down and see my sweet Maggie lying on the floor and my thoughts take yet another turn that I can't seem to shake. I start wondering if she knows just how ill she is. I wonder if she's hurting or scared. I wonder if she has any idea just how much I love her. I start welling up again knowing I can't stop the tears from falling.

How can the end be getting closer and closer? How do I say goodbye to someone who has been the equivalent to a child to me for over 14 years? Why can't I go through this for her? Why is it that at the end she has to go through this alone? Am I just giving myself a reason for a good cry? These kinds of questions keep running through my mind as I sit here in my quiet house.

I guess getting lost in thought has always been more of a passive activity for me, sort of like when I drive from my house to HEB (the local grocery store). I've been there a million times, so I'm pretty much on autopilot driving there. It's only when I arrive in the parking spot that I start questioning if all of those lights I just drove through actually were green. The difference now is that these thoughts aren't passive. They're very real, and, in this case, the reality sucks.

I have always had a knack for rambling on and on, so you could imagine what it must be like to be inside my head. Fortunately, after a few minutes, I find myself calming down as I help Maggie to bed. The rambling has subsided, but I know it is only temporarily silenced. I know the next time will catch me off guard again as my mind goes from passive to active thoughts. The floodgates have closed for the night, although I'm a bit emotionally drained.

I know in the morning I will do the same as I have done for the last several months. I will get up to let the dogs out and pray that when I open Maggie's door to her box that her chest is rising and falling in a relaxing slumber. Someday I know I'll awaken to an empty box, but for now I will cherish every day I have with her.

I will laugh at her crazy eyebrows. I will smile when I see her have a sudden burst of energy. I will continue to be generous with her treats and will look the other way when she decides to eat her brother's food instead of her own even though it's exactly the same. Most of all, I will remind myself that I will not love her for the rest of her life, but instead for the rest of mine.

Maggie was an amazing addition to my family. She didn't have a mean bone in her body. She brought so much joy to everyone who met her. I am forever grateful that I was by her side when she passed away. I was able to tell her I loved her, and I take comfort knowing it happened at home.

I was not so lucky with my other two dogs. One was attacked and killed in front of me while on a walk, and the other was hit by a car and killed about a year after my divorce. I often get lost in thought wondering what they were thinking at the end. Were they scared? Did they wonder why I didn't protect them? Did they know what was happening to them? These thoughts have passed through my mind so many times I've lost count, and one of my dogs died more than a decade ago.

What gives me peace is that I know I showed them love as if they were my children. I hope they know that they are thought of often and with many happy memories. They come to me sometimes in my dreams, and for just a little while, all is right with the world. I will miss them forever.

I Believe in the Fourth

As someone who has gone through the complete infertility roller coaster from the first diagnosis to the last failed attempt at in vitro fertilization, I found myself always dwelling on when life began. I know there are many opinions on this topic from a religious or political aspect, but go through what I've been through and you'll start to feel that life begins at conception. Especially during IVF, this moment can be very easy to detect from a doctor's perspective as it is done outside of the body. As some of you may know, last week a very dear friend passed away from cancer. I now find myself reflecting on a podcast I listened to a while back which discussed when a person is really considered dead, and it has helped me find some comfort.

When we're kids and someone passes away, many times we are given the generic answer that he or she is now in Heaven, and that usually suffices until we get a little older and realize how the human body works. Now, I'm no doctor, nor would I claim to be, but just as people have their views on when life begins, they too have an opinion on when life ends. There are three major ways most people view life ending: 1. when a person stops breathing 2. when a person's heart stops beating 3. when there is no brain activity. In my reflection this week, I have found that there is a fourth way and it is the one I believe in: 4. when a person is no longer spoken about.

I have lost many people and even pets in my life, but the one thing that keeps them alive for me is sharing my memories of them with others. I know that over the years, many friends and family members have witnessed our dear friend Frank and I doing the twist together at the occasional wedding or Bar/Bat Mitzvah. I'll talk about my sweet dog, Button, who was so scared trying to get away from a friend of mine that she ran inside my refrigerator. I picture my Bubbie (grandmother) telling my younger cousin (her grandson) who was a toddler at the time that she couldn't breastfeed him because she was "all dried up!" My husband and I recall his buddy Daryl visiting him in the computer lab while we were in college and, after watching him write some code, said, "Well that's just a bunch of letters and numbers and stuff."

Sure, I remember getting the news of their passing, or in Button's case witnessing it, but the point is that they are still talked about and still very much a part of my life. I just hope that if I can share my memories with enough people, then those I've lost because of one of the first three ways will never be lost because of the fourth.

It is when I recall a memory about a loved one who has passed that they appear to come back to life with such vividness, even if for just a split second. In some cases, I can picture them before me. Death is such an unknown for us all. We each have our beliefs about what happens, but I think what can be overwhelming at times is the fact that it is something you go through completely alone.

I have so many questions about this great mystery that I want answered, but I know that will only happen when I experience it myself. I think about my own life. I wonder how I will be remembered. Will others speak of me with fond memories? Will they speak of me kindly? Will they speak of me at all? I guess I simply hope my memory elicits feelings of love and happiness to all those whose lives I've touched. In the end, that's really all that matters.

Routines

I can still remember the hula hoop routine I performed to "New York, New York" in elementary school. I also remember the colorguard tryout routine to "Let's Dance" that I performed back in high school. Don't even get me started on Zumba…which is nothing but routines! So why does my brain work the way it does by allowing me to keep these things in my head long after I've needed them? Perhaps it's the repetition that went into learning each of them. It could also be that I find each of these events a little more significant and therefore feel the need to hold on to them. Regardless of the reasoning, I have found that I have always enjoyed learning routines.

It's nice to know what is coming next. There is something calming about knowing that there are no surprises. One move follows the next and so on. This is also the reason that I think I, and most other people, fall into a routine in our day-to-day lives. It might include how we get ready to go out. It may dictate the route we take in getting to a destination. Whatever the routine we come up with for the various parts of our lives, I believe they hold a special purpose…even when they are changed.

Many of the routines I have created serve as an internal checklist. For example, whenever I take a shower, I always follow the same routine: First, I shampoo my hair. Next, I wash my body and *then* face…and so on. I have a similar routine when I get out of the shower. There have been times that I'll begin a process and realize that I can't start one task because I never did the one that comes before it. This is my way of making sure I didn't forget something. I do the same thing when packing my toiletries for a trip. I always put the same things in the same location so that if something is missing I know to go grab it so it's not accidentally left behind.

What I have found over the years is that by being consistent with these routines, I rarely miss a step. Again, this prevents those unnecessary surprises that are caused by forgetting something. For example, imagine being a base jumper and not following some sort of routine in packing your gear before you take that final step off the edge. This process could be the last thing going through your mind when you've realized your chute didn't open properly. I'm thinking this would not be the time I'd want any sort of surprises!!

Something that I find very frustrating is when I'm in a situation that causes me to be outside of my normal routines. I can vouch that this can wreak havoc on a diet. I know from speaking with friends and family who have kids that it can also wreak havoc on a young child's sleep schedule. So then I have to ask myself, why do we do this to ourselves? Why do we go somewhere or do something that would prevent us from completing our normal routines?

Logic would tell us that it is inevitable. Unless we're in jail serving a life sentence, our day-to-day routine will eventually change due to a trip, a new job, or possibly our infamous Texas weather. Most of the time, I get comfortable in my routines, and it is only when I get outside my comfort zone that I find out how much I've relied on this structure in my life.

Fortunately, many routines can go with us. Just because I may not be in *my* shower doesn't change the steps I'll follow. I will still start with shampooing my hair, then grabbing the soap, and so forth. It is only when I return home that I get that sense of relief because now I can get back to my everyday routines.

Over the next few months I will be experiencing a myriad of events that will cause a change in my normal routines. The difference I find with myself now is that I am looking forward to these events. I look forward to the new memories I will make in the process. I look forward to the lessons I will learn, mostly about myself, during these times. I look forward to getting used to being outside the safety net of my comfort zone. It is only during times like these that I feel I can grow as a person.

I will discover new activities that interest me. I will find new ways of enjoying life. I will learn even more to appreciate that which is the day-to-day routine that I live by on a regular basis. Most of all, I will learn that change can be a good thing if I allow it to be.

I feel pretty confident in saying that I have taken many new and unexpected chances over the years. Some have been scary while others have been exciting. I'm continuing to grow as a person and believe now more than ever that I'm on a path that will lead to continued happiness. I'm finding my voice in many different ways and have ideas on how to challenge myself in the years to come. Life is an adventure, and I intend to see where it will take me.

It's Out of My Hands

I am the type of person who feels better when it appears I'm in control of a situation. When this occurs, I am rarely surprised by what is to come, as I am usually the one to make it happen. It's only when the whole illusion of control is taken away that I feel vulnerable, helpless, and unable to prepare for what's around the next corner. Many times, when something goes wrong, a person can be heard saying, "It's out of my hands." Sometimes this is because they feel as if they have done everything they could and are turning things over to a higher power. Other times it gives them the ability to distance themselves from what is happening, as it may appear there is no rhyme or reason for what has occurred.

I know I have said these words many times when going through infertility treatments. Whether it was the former or latter reason remains to be seen, but it did give me a sense of peace to speak those five little words. So yesterday, while on a run, I found myself pondering just how important our hands are and how there are usually two sides to everything that my hands have held.

Let me start with the basics. My hands have held *food*. As we all need food to survive, it is a necessary evil for someone like me who can very easily eat the wrong thing or, even worse, overeat. What is a constant struggle for me is that it is not someone else putting this food in my hands nor is it someone else putting the food into my mouth. *I* am the responsible one. What I eat is COMPLETELY in MY control, yet most of the time I feel out of control when I'm around it. Why is it that if I'm the one holding *it* that *it* is what has a hold on me? I can't not eat, so therein lies the conundrum.

Next, we'll move on to a little more complex topic. My hands have held *others' lives*. This may sound a bit dramatic, but this statement is true every time I get behind the wheel of a car…or in my case, Petey (my Expedition). It is my job to make sure that everyone in the vehicle gets from one destination to the next safely and without harm. The idea of being behind the wheel gives me the illusion that I am in control when in fact I am only partly. I have control, for the most part, of how my vehicle is driven as I decide the speed and maneuverability as I navigate my way around.

What is completely out of my control, and out of *my* hands, are the vehicles, objects, and weather around me. I don't know when someone will get distracted and run a red light. I have no way to know when the tire on the car in front of me will disintegrate and fly in my direction. I have no way to know that at one point in the road I will hit an unseen slick spot because of the rain and begin spinning across the next lane, the median, the oncoming traffic, and wind up on the opposite side from where I began. I can't expect someone to drive me everywhere, and to my knowledge no one has invented that handy-dandy teleporter yet, so again I face yet another conundrum.

Lastly, and most importantly, my hands have held *another's heart*. This may not be literally, but whether it be a dear friend, a family member, an infant, or a beloved pet, this is by far the most precious item I have been given the responsibility to hold. I've been blessed not only to welcome an infant just minutes after taking its first breaths, but I also comforted my sweet dog Button as she took her last. The amazing thing with holding someone's heart, whether human or not, is that they can simultaneously hold yours. If you are so lucky, it can even be held by multiple people at the same time.

What is in *our* control is whether we choose to nurture or neglect this prized possession. Once we give our heart to someone else, it is out of our hands what *they* choose to do with it. Remember, you can lead a horse to water, but you can't make it drink. Just because you have given someone your heart doesn't mean they will cherish it the way you do theirs. After all, we are all the sum of our experiences.

If all someone knows is hurt and anguish, then it will distort their view of your heart as if they are looking upon it with eyes in need of corrective lenses. From this standpoint, we do have control over one other thing…how we react to how others hold our hearts. Some people will want a loved one to hold on tighter while others would prefer they loosen their grip a little. Whatever the case, it is important to realize that this decision is out of our hands. That is the risk we all take when sharing our hearts with others.

As creatures on Earth, we have been blessed with the sense of touch. Although this is a physical act, it is when we are emotionally touched that we see the impact it has made on our lives. I think of everything I have touched and held thus far and what is yet to come. As I look down at my hands, I acknowledge the role they have played in how I see the world.

They have helped build homes and plant trees. They have comforted a friend during a difficult time and made a child giggle while playing peek-a-boo. They have opened doors to greet those who have stopped by for a visit and have closed doors as we have said our good-byes. They have wiped tears of joy and tears of sorrow and have typed and written words to convey to others how I am feeling.

I know that I have taken my hands for granted and should be more cognizant of just how important they have been and will continue to be during my life. When I think about what I have learned over the years, I hold on to the fact that the most important sense of all is in knowing that an open mind and an open heart will *always* come in handy.

Of all the things I've held on to in my life, the one thing that has had the most hold on me is my past. So often I look back on what's happened in my life and try to make sense of everything I've been through. What I've found is that the biggest change has come when I've learned that it really is okay to just let it go. This process has freed me up to embrace what's to come with open arms.

What do you want to be when you grow up? Think back to your childhood and try to imagine just how many times you were asked this question. Countless, I'm sure! When you're young, you truly believe you can be anything you can imagine. In many cases this is still true. If you work hard and apply yourself, you'll find that the sky's the limit. It's only when you get older that you realize that the careers of Superhero and Princess aren't really attainable...and they probably don't pay very well either. The other problem with these two careers is that you won't find them as a major in any college.

So now what? On average, a college student will change their major five times. I never actually changed mine...I just added a second major. For most college-bound people, though, they use this time to help them choose a path that will lead towards a future career. In some cases, it is only when you've graduated with your degree that you find you're not really sure exactly where this path is leading. I guess I would have fallen into this group.

I graduated from college with a Bachelor of Arts degree having double majored in Psychology and Communications. I even took an extra year and got my Secondary Teaching Certificate. Now, many years after completing my schooling, I find I am again searching for something I never truly found during my studies...direction.

We've probably all heard someone say at one point or another to do what you love and the money will follow. Either that or do what you love and you'll never work a day in your life. The way I see it, work is work. There's no getting around it. If you want something badly enough, it *has* to be worth working for. Lately, though, I feel like I've regressed back to my childhood. I've been asking myself the adult version of "What do I want to be when I grow up?" which, for me, sounds more like "What do I want to do with my life?" This is a pretty big question when you think about it.

Back in my early 20s after I was married, I began to rethink the whole "career" thing and felt that there was nothing more important than being a wife and mother. I felt like I had a pretty good grasp on the whole "wife" thing, but I *never* would have expected the second part of that career choice would be so difficult to attain.

So, I find myself in my mid-30s with no set career path feeling ridiculous when someone asks me what I do for a living. When I say I'm a stay-at-home wife, it is usually followed with one of those dreaded questions I've written about – "How many kids do you have?" – to which I have to answer "none." Sigh!!

I've realized that this is not the direction I expected my career to take. This path I have been on for the last few years has made me realize a few things. First, I need something more challenging in my life than seeing how many loads of laundry I can finish in a day. Next, on the days that I am busy, I don't eat nearly as much…mostly due to lack of boredom. Because of this, I figured finding a job will indirectly help me with my weight loss. Finally, if I'm going to find a career that truly makes me happy, then I'm going to have to step a bit out of my comfort zone.

After much consideration, I have made the decision to get certified to teach Zumba, which is a Latin-based dance fitness. This is something I enjoy, it helps me stay fit, and it's something I think other people can benefit from as well. Most importantly, it was *my* decision that has inspired me to travel down this new path, and I know I will only get out of it what I put into it. Where this endeavor will lead is a bit unclear right now, but I know it's a move in a new and different direction…and right now different is good!

73

The decision to get my Zumba certification has brought me so much joy over the years. First and foremost, I get to help others achieve their fitness goals through something as simple as dancing. It has given me a creative outlet in which to express myself and show a bit of my personality. I have taught a lot of classes over the years, and I'll admit that I got a bit burned out. This was something I was afraid of going into it, but the trade-off was so worth it. I have met so many incredible people, both men and women. I have seen the joy on their faces and watched their stress melt away. I have laughed with them and even cried with them. We have encouraged each other with high fives and applause. Most importantly, I have found a direction that gave more to me than I could possibly imagine. I still wonder sometimes what other amazing directions my life will take, but I can rest assured that I will always find my heart in music's beat.

Most of the time when something happens to us, we feel like no one else could *possibly* understand. We feel like this sort of thing could not *possibly* happen to someone else. We feel *alone*. What happens next is we either retreat inside ourselves or we look outside for someone who might identify with what we've been going through. Sure, most people deal with some sort of loneliness at one point or another, but knowing that we are *not* alone is always comforting.

A way of coping with these experiences is finding others who have something in common with you. This could range anywhere from having similar hobbies, liking the same kinds of foods, or even battling a disease. The possibilities are endless. What I have found is that joining one of these "clubs" is what helps me lessen my isolation.

Throughout my life, I've been a member of several clubs. I am proud to say I was a Girl Scout for 11 years and have so many wonderful memories of my time bonding with the other girls and, in most cases, their moms as well. Additionally, I am also fortunate to have been in the band and colorguard while in grade school and college and met many fun and talented people in those organizations.

It fascinates me to this day just how much of a bond you can have with someone who was in one of these two clubs growing up. You could have just met them and because you already have this in common, it serves as an ice breaker. Furthermore, like many other kids, I was a member of several soccer, t-ball, and softball teams growing up, and am still in touch with many of the people I played with way back when. The connections I have made with these people are harder to break, but as we all know, people can always grow apart.

Some of my deeper associations with people come from having

gone through profound, more emotional experiences. The very first blog I wrote talked about my struggle with infertility. I always have mixed feelings when I meet someone dealing with the same issues I have. While it isn't something you ever want to have in common with another person, it is definitely comforting knowing there is someone else who can relate to and empathize with your experiences.

This "club" of sorts reaches me on more of an emotional level than the traditional kind does. Members can read my first blog on "Surviving Those Questions and Comments" and understand exactly what I mean because they've experienced it firsthand. They know what I'm feeling and why I'm feeling it without me having to explain anything. Being a member of the same religion or race falls under this category as well. For example, I was raised as a Jewish woman living in the Bible Belt. Unless you are a fellow Jew and lived and grew up where I did, you wouldn't even begin to understand the feelings of segregation that go along with being in the religious minority. You wouldn't understand what it's like to have to sing songs about Jesus because your school is putting on a Christmas play and you don't have a choice but to participate…unless you want to feel even more isolated than you already do. How many of those of you who are married can say that you were the first person of your religion that your spouse met? I can! I guess he liked Jewish people. ;-) Thinking about these "clubs," I realize that they are the kind that you hope has very few members.

We all want to feel like we belong…somewhere. We spend most of our lives trying to find our place in this universe. Where do we fit in? What is our purpose? Why are we here? I have discovered that many times the answers to these questions come from fitting into one of our "clubs." Maybe I was meant to go through my difficult experiences so I could help someone else work through the same issues. Maybe my struggles were meant to teach someone else just how blessed they really are when their life seems overwhelming.

Perhaps my place in the cosmos is to help someone understand that differences in people are a good thing. Remember, you're a unique person…just like everyone else. After reading all of this, if you feel more confused about your life than when you started…well…join the club!

Each club in my life has taught me something very valuable. Girl Scouts taught me to leave a place or situation in better condition than how I found it. Band and colorguard taught me that while the whole is greater than its individual parts, it is the individual who has to do his or her part for the group to be successful as a whole. Infertility and divorce taught me again and again that you never know how strong you CAN be until you HAVE to be. These weren't always easy lessons to learn, but their value is definitely worth the dues I've paid.

Friendship

I can't imagine my life without my friends. Moreover, I wouldn't want to. Just knowing there are people out there who can make me smile, who know my heart, who are there to listen, and who love me unconditionally is more comforting than I can possibly explain. I've had such unique experiences with so many people in my life, some that even date back to when I was living in Cincinnati. In recent conversations with a few friends, I started thinking back to how long I've known them, and in many cases it was longer than we had realized. In all my years, the one thing I've learned is that in order to have good friends, you have to be a good friend first. So what does it mean to me to be a friend? To me, I think of the four Ls.

Loving unconditionally

This concept is not an easy one for many people, as they cannot do the same for themselves. In some cases, it takes someone showing you unconditional love before you can truly understand it. To be able to be yourself, your whole self, and know that your relationship with another person will not end regardless of what mistakes you may make can be a very cathartic feeling. It's easy to judge another person. Unless you have lived your life free from mistakes, what you tend to learn is that it may be easy to dish out the judgments, but it's not so easy to take them when they're aimed back at you.

Listening

When most people engage in conversations, they tend to do the same thing. Instead of really *hearing* what someone is saying, they instead only pay attention to the first few words of what was spoken. This in turn causes them to begin thinking of what they are going to say in response, followed by them doing so. To be a good friend, you really have to learn to take notice of what is said, and in some cases, what *isn't* said. Being present in the conversation is vital. Learning to just simply shut up can do wonders for a relationship, especially when it is obvious the other person just needs to be heard without interruption.

Laughing

Imagine your life for one moment without joy, pleasure, or even a simple smile. It's not really something I'd like to envision. I thoroughly enjoy making others happy. I won't say I'm *always* a "glass is half full" kind of gal, as everyone can have a bad day from time to time. I guess I'd like to think that more often than not, I am. Laughing with someone is such a great way to show a person that they are accepted and loved. More importantly, learning to laugh at *yourself* can go a long way to make others feel at ease.

Learning to forgive

Mistakes are a part of life. Show me a person who has not messed up at one point or another and I will show you someone who is still in diapers. The most selfless thing you can do for a friend is to offer them forgiveness. The act of forgiving goes along with loving someone unconditionally. You cannot have one without the other.

Remember that everyone is fighting some sort of battle, and for many, they may feel like they are fighting it alone. Knowing that there are allies that will be there to stand by them in their moments of need can make the difference between winning and losing. Friends may come into your life for a reason, a season, or a lifetime. Whatever the case is for each person I've met throughout my life thus far, I know that I am better person for knowing each of you. I *always* learn a little more about myself in the process of getting to know someone, and I am truly grateful for each of these lessons, as it gives me a little more ammo to help me fight *my* battles.

I'd have to say that friendship is one of the best inventions ever...along with family and chocolate. These relationships, however, are not without their challenges. The give and take that makes up a friendship has to be balanced, and it has to be done together or it just won't work. Over the years, I've learned two very important lessons: When someone wants to walk out of your life, let them, and when someone shows you who they really are, believe them. These lessons don't mean that I was a bad friend to them, but knowing when to walk away can be a way of being a friend to yourself.

Own It!

A few years ago, I went to work for my neighbor who had started a company out of his home. Having never worked in that particular industry, I wasn't sure exactly how to go about completing certain tasks he gave me. When I asked him how to do something one day, his response kind of pissed me off. He simply said, "Own it!" Ummm…okay. What I didn't realize until a few months later was that that was some of the best advice I've ever gotten.

Those two tiny words taught me that as an adult, I need to figure things out on my own. If it becomes my instinct to go to someone every time I try something new, then I'm never going to grow as a person. There are many things we do in life that require us to learn independently. What I have found is that when we are given the chance to do so, we tend to get more out of this independent learning than just an answer to our immediate question.

In the spring of 1990, I decided to try out for the colorguard at my high school and follow in my sister's footsteps. I remember being in the backyard at my parents' house trying over and over again to do the most basic move – a drop spin. My sister was outside with me at the time spinning one of her rifles. I was getting very frustrated because every time I would do a drop spin, my flag would roll up. After a few frustrating minutes of this, I finally asked my sister what I was doing wrong. Her advice was priceless. She told me, "Just figure out what you're doing and then don't do it anymore!" GENIUS!! Of course, at the time, I was NOT her biggest fan, and am sure the look on my face communicated that clearly!! I may have wanted to throw my flag at her at the moment, but, by saying that, it made me work harder and pay attention to exactly what I was doing. Lo and behold, I not only figured it out, but my junior and senior years I was the colorguard captain.

Moments like these have made a large impact on who I am today. I don't tend to wait around for someone to show me how to do something, but rather I start off trying to figure it out on my own. Many times I will discover something in addition to what I was trying to accomplish, whether it be a shortcut in a program or a faster way of doing something, but regardless, it is probably something I wouldn't have learned had I just had someone feed me the answer.

Don't get me wrong, I do have enough sense to know when asking questions is warranted *prior* to beginning a task or project. There have been many occasions that, looking back, I *should* have asked questions…LOTS of questions, but didn't. In most cases, those situations resulted in a ton of wasted time on my part and in some cases a lot of money as well. Many of you have heard me talk about Petey. He is my Expedition, and he's been with us since 2000, although he's a 1997 model. We were in need of a different car at the time because my husband was unable to drive our Ford Ranger from San Antonio to Austin each day prior to us moving here because we couldn't go over the miles on our lease. Instead, he was driving my cute little Ford Escort Station Wagon. Talk about a comfy drive for someone who is 6'2"! Anyway, while visiting my in-laws one weekend, we took a trip into San Angelo to look for a used vehicle. This is where I fell in love with Petey.

We didn't want to be taken advantage of at a car dealership (I know, imagine that!), so we had decided ahead of time how much we could afford for a monthly payment. We sat down with the sales guy and, thinking we were showing him who was boss, we said that we wanted *that* car for *this* monthly payment. If he could do that for us, we would drive away with it today! I'm sure you can guess…he met our price!!! He did this by increasing the number of months that we would have to pay out the note, which meant the price of the vehicle went up! We didn't care! We got the car we wanted at the monthly price we asked for!

It wasn't until a few months later that we did the math and figured out just how screwed we were. Sure, this was an expensive mistake, but it was definitely a "learning experience." Have we made that same mistake again? Nope!...of course we haven't bought another vehicle since then, but I'm afraid that time may be quickly approaching.

Looking back over all my experiences in life, I have learned a surplus of lessons. Sure, most of them I've learned the hard way...the *very* hard way, but the point is that I *learned* something. Had I not been given the opportunity to discover these things in my own way, I wouldn't be the person I am now. Think about what your life would be like if you didn't figure out how to pick yourself back up after a devastating or frustrating experience. What if you had always been given the answers and didn't have to learn to think for yourself? Remember, there is a thin line between knowing when to give up and knowing when to try harder. To truly know which is the correct path can only come from experience.

I still live by these words today. I'm constantly challenged in my profession, but I realize each time something new is thrown at me that it's just something I haven't yet mastered. Challenge accepted!

I share something in common with the following people: Bill Clinton, Richard Simmons, H.G. Wells, Martina McBride, M.C. Escher, Oprah Winfrey, Monica Seles, and Jason Kabakoff (my brother). All of the people listed above are fellow southpaws. Yes that's *right*, I'm a lefty…in case you didn't already know.

I've had many experiences in my life that have forced me to look at things differently. Being raised Jewish living in the Bible Belt has been a challenge, to say the least. Having to spell both my first and last names (maiden and married) for people has often made me wish I could just go by my initials at times. The one thing, however, that has been both a blessing and a curse is being left-handed.

Most people go through life not thinking twice about some everyday item they use or something as mundane as driving to work. These people are right-handed. Imagine trying to use a pair of scissors in a way that is comfortable for you only to find you have to switch hands because they DON'T WORK OTHERWISE! In order to drive a car, the ignition, gear shift, and accelerator all require either the use of your right hand or foot.

When signing your name on the credit card machine at the store, many times they can't be turned so that a lefty can use it without it looking like your signature was done upside down with your eyes shut. Don't even get me started with the writing on pens that is *always* upside down when I'm trying to read it or the coffee mugs that always have the witty saying on the wrong side. Three-ring binders physically hurt unless you take the page out first before writing on it. Then when you do start writing, you end up smearing everything you've written…especially on a dry erase board! These are just a few of the examples of the day-to-day fun I have as one of yet another minority.

After all these years, I've come to embrace my lefty-ness and especially to have more of a sense of humor when it comes to it. I once saw a funny sign at a store that has a man with his arm all contorted trying to fill out a form of some sort that said, "Hire left-handed people because it's funny to watch them write." It still cracks me up to watch a right-handed person cut their meat at a meal. It seems like such a waste of time to switch their fork and knife when cutting only to switch it back when they are ready to eat. I'm not saying all right-handed people do this, but those who don't are few and far between.

I also tend to notice more often than my non-lefty friends and family when someone I've either met or seen on television are members of the handedness minority. This trait came in really handy (pun intended) when I was in colorguard in high school and college. Because *I* am more dominant on my left, and most of the moves in colorguard are done using the *right* hand, I was able to perform with ease many of the same moves on both sides. This was especially helpful when teaching a routine or move to someone. Because I could face them doing it "backwards" in a sense, I would end up mirroring them, allowing them an easier time for them to grasp what I was teaching.

What I have found is that most lefties tend to adapt to doing something that requires a bit of ambidextrousness a little easier than others do. I will never forget going to see my niece (who is right-handed) and noticing that she had only the nails on her left hand painted. When I asked her why she didn't paint the rest of her nails, she said it was because she couldn't paint them with her left hand. I got a good laugh out of that one!

I know that statistics show that left-handed people live an average of seven years less than their right-handed counterparts, and it's no wonder with all the dangerous things out there that could trip us up. Because we expect that we'll have to adapt more often than not, I think it gives us a little more of an edge in avoiding the hazards. For example, I know that unless you buy one specially made, a bolt-action rifle is set up for a right-handed person. Additionally, most power tools and gardening tools are made for the majority…and before you start to wonder, yes I have used both and have found them a challenge. There's nothing like having the sawdust blown in your face because you're using the tool on *your* terms. I can see how this could pose a threat to someone who hasn't listened to good old Norm Abram's safety speech!

I guess I'd have to say that the unique thing about this "club" is that you can only become a member if you are born this way or if for some reason you lose the use of your right hand. It's not like converting to another religion or changing your hair color after all. I wouldn't think it's something that you would just choose to do on a whim. I look forward to the day when being a lefty gives me the advantage as opposed to the disadvantage over someone else. Of course, when all is said and done, I can look back on this unique trait I've inherited and rest easy knowing that most people may be born right-handed, but only the gifted overcome it!

I'll be honest. Being left-handed is pretty great. I like knowing that I have a trait that makes me unique. It's sort of like knowing my middle name has a "z" in it. Not many people have a "z" in their name. What I find amusing is that upon telling someone I'm left-handed, they usually respond with a resounding, "Really?!" That always makes me laugh because I wonder if anyone has ever lied about being left-handed. Well, as I often say, we are the only ones in our right minds.

Epiphanies

There are probably very few people who can tell you their favorite sound. I am not one of those people. I know what mine is! My favorite sound can be heard when someone who has been trying to figure something out for a while finally has a breakthrough. What follows next is pure music to my ears... "Ohhhh!!" We've all had one of those moments...hopefully! It really does happen more frequently than you might think. Maybe you just haven't listened for it before, but something tells me you might notice it moving forward. There is another type of breakthrough that you can have that may or may not result in you expressing my favorite sound, but it doesn't make it any less substantial. What I am referring to is an epiphany.

Epiphanies can occur at any age. A good example of one at a very early age is the realization that the baby in the mirror is not another person but instead just a reflection of yourself. As we age, these experiences mature with us. Sure, most teenagers think they know everything and their parents couldn't possibly understand what they are going through. I know I felt that way at that age. What I discovered was that early in my twenties I came to understand that my parents have been through much of the same life lessons as I had at that point and maybe I should start listening to their advice. Maybe I should learn from *their* experiences.

I've done my best to keep this in mind throughout the years and I think that overall, I have. Because of it, I am more likely to ask their advice *prior* to tackling something new rather than after I've already screwed it up.

As we get into our later adulthood and have learned many of the difficult lessons life has thrown our way, the epiphanies that we have can stop us in our tracks. In these moments of clarity, I find the answer to the question that I have been asking myself for a while…Why? Why am I always making the same mistake when it comes to one issue? Why am I having such difficulty dealing with this situation? Why does it bother me so much when I'm treated a certain way by a certain person?

Sometimes these answers come to me while I'm driving somewhere. Sometimes they come to me while I'm exercising. I can even remember a time I had an epiphany in the middle of a Weight Watchers meeting.

So, what is it about our brains at the time that allow for this moment of great revelation? Are we just relaxed enough mentally that what was trying to get out finally does? Is it a sign from above that the answer to our prayers has finally arrived? Is it just dumb luck? Who knows?!

The important thing is that whatever aligned in our world to allow us to come to the much-needed conclusion put us in a better frame of mind and moves us along in our forward progression as a human being. Here's looking forward to each of your next "Ohhhh!" moments…and the hopes that I might be there to experience the music that only an instant like that can produce!

This favorite sound of mine is so satisfying. It's almost as if it brings out the inner cheerleader in me. I'm always so excited for the person who uttered it. I get doubly excited when that person is me! Sometimes in life we have to celebrate the little things…such as when you finally remember why you got up off the couch and walked into the kitchen.

There are few things that truly catch me off-guard. For the most part I find that my life is fairly predictable. I go through my day-to-day routines with a little bit of variation here and there, but usually it's nothing I can't handle. Of everything I deal with on a regular basis, it is my emotional state that can throw me for a loop in a split second and can last until either I fall asleep or something or someone snaps me out of it. I understand that emotions are there to help you deal with what life throws your way, but there are times when I feel like I am a one-woman team in a lopsided game of dodgeball.

Like many people, I'll cry at a sad movie. I'll laugh at a funny joke. I *always* get nervous before getting on a roller coaster. What fascinates me is how my body reacts to what I'm experiencing. I never thought about the *why* of emotion, as it's something that most of us take for granted. Unless you're an actor…or trying to get out of a speeding ticket…you don't have to work at crying, as it is something that just happens naturally. But how does this really work? How does your body know that each time you feel sad, the correct physiological reaction is to cry and frown? When you're happy, how does it know to smile and laugh? Obviously, it was most likely a learned reaction as we watched others do this before us. So, what about the first person to cry?

All my life, I've never really felt like I've been able to control my emotions as well as others. I guess I just tend to wear my heart on my sleeve and can find that something that might not affect the average person can be intensified by how *I* react to it. There are so many times that I wish I could just turn off my emotions. Whether it be from me trying to tell a joke that I can't make it through without cracking up (thanks for passing down that trait, Dad!!) or losing someone I've come to care about very much, I often think how much easier it would be not to feel so strongly. What would it be like to be able to just turn off my feelings temporarily? Just imagine not being lonely, depressed, bored, or even frustrated. Sure, it would most likely lead to a downturn in our society, as it is emotions like compassion and empathy that help us learn right from wrong.

Regardless of this, because of how strongly my emotional response can be, a break from feeling, even for a few minutes, would be very welcome at times. I'm not talking about turning it off so I could commit a crime, as I'm too stupid (or maybe too smart) to be a criminal. I just mean during those times that things seem overwhelming and some emotional distance would help me see the big picture a little more clearly, it might just come in handy.

From the time we're born, we begin developing our fascination with everything around us as we experience things for the first time. I think what is important is that we never lose that sense of curiosity. After all, it was once said, "Curiosity was framed. Ignorance killed the cat." It is most likely for this reason that I continue to write and learn, and most of all to truly experience what comes my way. Life was never guaranteed to be easy, but it is what we make of it...at least that's how I *feel*.

Several years back, while going through a very difficult time, I went to see my doctor, and we both agreed that I could benefit from a mild antidepressant. This wasn't a permanent fix, but rather it was just something to get me "over the hump." I just couldn't seem to get my emotions in check and found myself crying quite often. As the medicine took effect, I noticed myself level out a bit. This was a huge relief and a nice change from the days and days of unprovoked tears...or so I thought.

It was about 10 months later that I gained a bit of perspective on my own life. I realized that there was a reason I was crying before, but now, the medicine I was on would not give me the emotional release I needed. My point was, I couldn't cry, and I needed to at that point. Working with my doctor again, we weaned me off the medication, and I was able to make it through my day-to-day life much stronger than when I started. When I wrote about wanting to turn off my emotions, I didn't really understand just how frustrating that can be. There is a reason I was feeling the way I did. There is a natural reaction that your body goes through when this happens.

I'm not saying that I didn't need the medication, but I feel different now. I still wear my heart on my sleeve, and it can be a struggle at times. The difference is, I allow myself to feel the emotion without thinking something is wrong with me. It's like a gut feeling. I guess I've learned to trust my emotional gut, and, so far, it hasn't steered me wrong.

Boy Am I Glad I Learned English First!

Throughout my life I've been fortunate to have the chance to learn a few different languages. I've taken Spanish lessons, been taught a little bit of sign language (yes, I count that!!), and I can even read and write Hebrew…although I can't translate it. Maybe someday I'll even take Italian, as I've always found it to be a very romantic language. Of all the foreign languages out there, I would have to say that I am SO GLAD I learned English *first*!!

I have always been a fan of grammar, oftentimes getting out my virtual "red pen" when I'm perusing posts on Facebook or reading an email. I remember having fun taking a test when I applied for my position at USAA. The test was simply a paragraph with every few words separated by lines and an "R" and "W" underneath for right and wrong. You had to look at spelling, punctuation, capitalization, etc. and determine if that segment was written correctly. That may have been the only test in my life I've taken with a big grin on my face. Yes, I know I'm a sick person! ;-)

Many parts of the English language have baffled me for years. First and foremost is the alphabet!! It seems to me that this list can be condensed by deleting a few of the letters we really don't need. For example, we really don't need a "c." We have an "s" and a "k" that can cover both of the sounds this letter makes when part of a word. Next, there's the letter "x" which can be replaced by "eks" or "z." It's not used all that often anyways, so who will really miss it?!? Additionally, I would like to say sorry to Elizabeth, but we really don't need a "q" either. Can we not spell her title as "Kween" instead? This brings me to another point about the letter "q." Why is it that the cursive version of this letter looks like a floppy 2? Maybe that's how the term "tween" came about.

Let's move on, shall we?

What kind of stupid language is written so that in order to pronounce a word correctly you have to read the words around it?!? "He wanted to record a record." Ummmm…wait…let me read (present tense) that again so I don't sound like an idiot in 5th grade in front of the whole class when I mispronounce not only one, but both of those words.

One of my biggest pet peeves about this language is the use of contractions. I have lost count of how many times this part of grammar has been trampled on each and every day. It fascinates me how a little thing like an apostrophe can confuse even the smartest person. The groups of words that drive me nuts include "they're/their/there," "your/you're," "its/it's," "were/we're," and "y'all." Just to clear up, that last word is made up of the words you and all, not ya and ll.

I've often thought what it would be like to try to learn English at my age. There are so many stupid rules to remember. I still have trouble spelling after all these years and even catch myself reciting "i before e except after c" whenever I can't remember which one comes first. Then just when you think you're safe, here comes trying to master "fun with plurals!" Why is the plural of mouse mice, but the plural of house isn't hice?!? Oxen? Correct. Boxen? NOPE!! Why can't you just add an "s" to the end of every word and be done with it?!? Also, another issue I have with this crazy language includes why the word *building* can be both a noun *and* a verb!! Furthermore, why do you drive in a parkway and park in a driveway?! SHEESH!! Apparently rules in English are meant to be broken.

Finally, let's discuss some other parts of the English language that tend to rake on my nerves. Why on Earth is the word *abbreviation* so long? Why is it that the word *daughter* and *laughter* don't rhyme? Why does the word *vacuum* need two u's in it?! That could be remedied by using "yoo" to make the word *vakyoom*. Looks much better to me! Then there are homophones and homonyms. Homophones are those words that sound the same but are usually spelled differently and have *completely* different meanings. Examples of these include hare/hair, led/lead, and but/butt. In each of *these* cases, there is only a difference of one letter to make a world of difference in the meaning. Were there really not enough letters to come up with a whole new word?! Homonyms are those words that are spelled the same but have different meanings. Imagine the different between these two sentences: "He runs." versus "He has the runs." BIG difference!!

I know that every language has its quirks, but it seems to me that whoever came up with English didn't do a good job of thinking things through. Haven't they heard the notion of keeping it simple? Less is more? I guess what I've realized in my quest to understand this crazy language is that the only thing that makes sense is that *IT* doesn't.

This continues to amaze me, especially in our world of texting, autocorrect, and social media. It really seems to me that, as a society, we have dumbed down our communication. Why have our standards dropped to being okay with these crimes against our language?! I am CONSTANTLY refraining from correcting people on a daily basis because I don't want to be THAT person. I guess I'm of the minority who still uses correct grammar and punctuation while emailing and texting. My sister actually bought me a mug that reads, "I'm silently correcting ~~you're~~ your grammar." She knows me too well! I would say I wish I didn't care about all of this, but the truth is, I do...very much so. I just wish other people did as well.

Time

For some reason I tend to notice when a clock reads "12:34" more than any other time. Maybe it's because I think those numbers in order are more interesting than any other time or maybe I just don't pay attention otherwise. Regardless, I've found that time is a funny thing. It can make you forget some things while aiding you in remembering others. It helps to heal wounds, emotional and otherwise, or can open new ones when you realize it took a mistake of a fraction of a second to change someone's life forever. Time can fly when you want something to last longer, or it can seem to drag on and on especially when you're bored. You can look forward towards the future with optimism or reflect back on the past with regret. In the end, how time passes depends on someone's perspective.

A very wise person recently told me that a person's perception is their own reality. So if our reality is in our heads, then does time only exist in our brains? Does it pass more quickly for a fruit fly that has a short life cycle or does its perspective allow time to pass more slowly considering it's a lifetime's worth of experiences?

We've all heard the phrase "stop and think about it," but we know we can't stop time from passing. No matter how much fun we're having or how tragic a loss we experience, the world keeps spinning. Maybe if we had a time machine, we could go back and fix the mistakes of our past or spend a little while longer reliving those moments that seemed to fly by back in the day. This possibility would completely dissolve the idea of living for the moment.

What consequences would we have then for making any decision now if later we could just go back for a do-over? Would that make us a better society or a more devious one? This could be dangerous in the wrong person's hands. Imagine a criminal going back in time to clean up that evidence that got him caught in the first place. How many crimes would then go unpunished? On the flip side, how many time would we like to go back to a first date and do something differently?

Furthermore, is living for the present supposed to represent a day, an hour, a minute, a second, etc.? Is it really possible to live for the present as the present instantly becomes the past? Are we in reality really living for the past? Are we just trying to live so that our happiness and good choices outweigh our sorrow and regrets? I guess only time will tell!

I really enjoy watching shows about space and am fascinated with its vastness. I have looked up at the night sky and witnessed the amazing display of stars that blanket every corner. What I find incredible is just how far away these celestial bodies are from Earth and how far the light has had to travel. Because of this, I am looking at the light as it was thousands, millions, or maybe billions of years ago. Even the light from my reflection takes time to get from the mirror to my eyes. Because of this, I am aware that I am constantly looking at things in the past.

So I am constantly asking myself, how do I think about the future when all I see is the past? I don't know how the choices I make now will affect my future. What if I turned right instead of left? Do each of these miniscule choices push me in one direction towards an alternate future that is less than ideal? There's just no way to know. Time will pass regardless, so all I can do is make my decisions, learn from their outcomes, and continue to move forward.

The Unseen Struggle

I am the sum of my experiences. They make me who I am. The tough times I've been through shape how I view the world. They shape how I react to what someone says or does. No one else has walked a mile in my shoes or survived what I have. That part of me, the part that changed me forever due to struggle or tragedy, is invisible.

There isn't a physical scar acting as a symbol of what I've endured. Hell, looking at me you wouldn't know that I'm a lefty…or Jewish-ish…or a Yankee. What's more, looking at me you have no way to know that I've been through infertility treatments, been divorced after a 16+ year marriage, struggle all day every day with food and food-related issues, or am incredibly lonely. My damage is unseen.

It hides behind a smile. It takes no physical shape and does not leave a physical scar. The hurt is much deeper. It has dulled quite a bit over the years, but it's still there. Certain things can trigger it and bring it to the surface. I'm learning to be kinder to myself and more forgiving towards others when their benign actions or words create a reaction in me that is due to years of hurt.

I'm trying to remember that if I am dealing with this kind of unease within me then so is everyone else. My battle may be very different from yours, but it's still there, and I'm learning to remember that being kind is important, both to others and to myself. Uncloaking and revealing my wounds to someone can be very scary, but moving forward in the face of fear is what I intend to do.

There are times that I wished there was some sort of marker to show what I've been through without asking, just like an avatar in a video game. I wonder if people would speak more kindly to each other if they could tell with a glance exactly what battles those around them are fighting. Maybe that person at the grocery store or in the car in front of you in traffic wouldn't annoy you as much. It can be difficult to be forgiving when you don't know the motivation behind someone's actions.

The Safety of the Street Light

Whenever I misplaced something growing up, my dad would always tell me that, "it will always be in the last place you look." Gee…thanks, Dad! After all, who would keep looking after they found what they were seeking? What about the person who is searching for something nowhere near where they lost it just because it's easier? It doesn't make much sense, does it? This is what is known as the Streetlight Effect.

This can best be described by a short story about a drunk man who has lost his keys. He is standing under a street light trying to find them when a police officer walks up and asks him what he is looking for. Upon telling the officer what he lost, they both begin searching together for the keys. After several minutes of looking, the officer asks the drunk man if he's sure he lost them there. The drunk man points across the street into the darkness and tells the officer that he lost his keys over there in the park. The police officer asks him why he's searching here, to which the drunk man replies, "This is where the light is."

I pondered this for a while and wondered why we try to find the easy way out in life? Why do we search for answers in the wrong places? Why do we want the "get rich quick" scheme to work instead of focusing our efforts towards the target we're trying to reach? It feels lately as if someone has discovered me crouched under a street light searching for what I seek most – happiness.

Sure, trying to be happy with what you have and what you're already doing is a good thing, but *trying* and *being* are two completely different things. After all, wouldn't you rather spend time doing some real soul searching if it meant you would find what you seek? Wouldn't it be worth it to step away from the view and safety beneath your street light in order to find your keys to happiness?

99

Remember what my dad said – you'll always find what you seek in the last place you look. It's a good thing I'm smart enough to grab my flashlight.

Part of finding happiness with yourself is discovering who you are and what you really want in life. I have never heard of this being a short or straight road for anyone, but finding what you seek is worth the search.

There was a time when I was so out of shape I couldn't jog longer than about 30 seconds without feeling like my heart was going to burst out of my chest. I remember wanting someday to be able to get to the point where I could run a 5K. That goal seemed so unattainable that I never thought it would happen. I'm happy to say that, since that time, I've run many 5Ks, and earlier this year completed a half marathon, although I walked the second half due to my knees revolting for putting them through that insanity.

For many people who have never considered themselves a runner, there are tools out there that will walk you through going from getting your tushy off your couch to crossing the finish line of one of a number of races. It got me thinking after listening to a podcast during my morning drive the other day if there would be some sort of similar route to allow a "regular person" to go from their couch to being an Olympian.

I would think that the first thing you must consider is what skills do you already have in your athletic arsenal that would get you to the end goal as quickly as possible. Do you already enjoy running? Are you able to leap tall horizontal beams in a single bound? Can you ski the K-12 with a kid on a bike chasing you? If so, you may be closer to the end goal than most.

I started thinking about what events I could work towards without the fear of being laughed at during the Olympic trials. What I found was there were a multitude of ones that I don't have a snowball's chance in hell of competing in that it made me giggle. Here is what I came up with:

    1. Water Polo & Synchronized swimming – Both of these require hours of treading water. That in itself seems so

exhausting that I had to take a nap upon this realization.

2. Fencing – Just the thought of not being able to use the line, "I am not left-handed," (since I am) or not having a competitor who is looking for the six-fingered man would be a total letdown.

3. Sailing – Considering that I still get spooked jumping off a diving board into the deep end and expecting Jaws to attack me from below makes me realize that purposely putting myself in that very situation would not be the wisest decision.

4. Diving – See #3. Plus, potentially ending my practice or competition with a belly flop or back buster is reason enough to avoid this one altogether.

5. Cycling (of any sort) – Until they make a bicycle seat made out of a bean bag chair, you won't catch me on one anytime soon. I think my derriere still hurts from the last time I went for a ride, and that was well over a year ago.

6. Archery – I know my name is spelled with a "y," but I don't want to risk forever being called Robyn Hood.

I guess my chance of being a contender in the competitions already in place are quickly dwindling. Here are some fictional Olympic events that I could confidently say would result in me standing atop the highest podium while listening to our amazing national anthem being played:

1. Pantry Organizing – OK…so this would really be any organizing event – pantry, drawers, computer files, party plans, etc. I'd probably have a devilish grin on my face the whole time. That should make for some great pics for my Wheaties box debut.

2. Coloring Inside the Lines – It is my attention to detail that gives me the upper hand in completing this event successfully and leaving my competition in the dust.

3. Picture Leveling – Considering that my superhero name

is "The Level-er," I have no doubt that few could compete with my ability to ensure that a frame is both level and plumb. This could also morph into desk arrangement, as it is only logical to have everything at 90-degree angles, hence the term "right" angles. Everything else is just wrong.

4. Random Fact, Movie Line, & Song Lyrics Quoter – If you ask me if I remember what I learned in college, you will find that it is not the book learning that I can easily recall, but rather the little tidbits of useless information that serve no real purpose. Furthermore, I'd have to say that while humans use a small portion of our brain capacity, mine is probably 99% full of this kind of information, some of which is very obscure. The best part about this event is that as you're competing, you're adding even more useless knowledge to your collection. Why have they not started this?!?!

So, who's with me? It's time we put our talents to good use, encourage some patriotism, and win the gold for the USA!!

I've always wondered how I'll leave my mark on this world. I have no doubt that it will not include an Olympic medal, so we can mark that off the list with confidence. We each have our own talents. Some of mine tend to surprise people, like the fact that I can juggle three tennis balls at a time. Maybe that will be my legacy. No...not juggling, but rather having just enough random talents to keep people surprised. I could live with that.

Time flies. It's about time. There's not enough time in the day. It seems that we all have time on our minds, especially since we just lost an hour due to daylight saving time…well most of the nation, at least. I've been thinking about it a lot lately. I think back to where I've been personally, professionally, and even geographically, and I often catch myself wondering where I'll be in another year. What new friends will I have made? Will I travel to any new places? More importantly, what new lessons will I have learned? That's what fascinates me about time: the possibilities are infinite.

Now, I'll be the first to admit that I'm a geek. I had a great time celebrating Super Pi Day on March 14th. For those who aren't aware (or who don't geek out over stuff like this as I do), this was the last time for 100 years that 3/14/15 will show up on a calendar. I even snapped a picture on my iPhone at 9:26 am. That's right…3.1415926!!! See…I'm a geek!! :-)

I had an even crazier, almost star-struck moment a week ago when a replica of the *Back to the Future* DeLorean pulled up next to me at the gas station. I was squealing with excitement as I saw the flux capacitor fluxing, the time circuits working, and even the Mr. Fusion affixed to the back. It was absolutely AMAZING!!! I snapped several pics as I had the greatest conversation with the owner, his girlfriend or wife, and their *adorable* Boston Terrier, Tesla (GREAT NAME!!). It wasn't until a few days later that I had a crazy time epiphany based on this chance encounter.

See if you can follow me on this one. FYI…you MUST picture me saying this with my eyes WIDE OPEN and my eyebrows raised as high as my facial muscles will allow.

WHAT IF that was the ACTUAL time-traveling DeLorean from 1985 that had come 30 years into the future…just like in the movie?!?! Maybe they've already had some experiences with Texas weather changing on a dime, as it did in the second movie of the trilogy. When they go *back* to 1985, they decide it might be interesting to pitch their movie idea to some people in Hollywood. The movie gets made using their DeLorean as the prototype for the time machine and they simply change the name and breed of the dog to protect the identity of the real one. Now OF COURSE the scene where they meet some crazy, star-struck woman at a gas station gets cut because in the grand scheme of things it really is a blip on the overall visit to the future. Nonetheless, it is TOTALLY possible!!

...or is it?!?!

I've long been a fan of all things geek. This includes astronomy, astrophysics, and, of course, time travel. As you could imagine, it's one thing to travel through time, but you're also traveling through space. Just because you go back 30 years, it doesn't mean the Earth is going to be in the same relative location as it was before. You have to remember, we are not just moving around the sun, but we are moving through the Milky Way galaxy. If you travel back in space and time, or spacetime, you're at risk of ending up in a wall, on the other side of the Earth, or even out in space itself. I don't even want to *try* to contemplate the math on that one!

Sure, we're all at the mercy of a clock in one way or another. We check it when we wake up, it mocks us when we're running late to work or an appointment, and it seems to speed up when we're enjoying ourselves. Despite our best efforts to slow things down, time keeps ticking away. It's as if we were given a bank account and in it are the seconds, minutes, and hours of our lives. We can't make deposits, only withdrawals. I guess the real question is, since we know the account will eventually be depleted, what is the best way to spend our time?

It's things like this that gets my brain going in a million different directions. I hope this fascination and wonder continues throughout my life and possibly rubs off on others.

As a single woman, I find myself on occasion lost in thought. This could be while driving, during an afternoon walk, or while at home relaxing on the couch. I'm sure that normal daydreaming is healthy, and I'll admit that I've done my share. Every so often I notice something somewhat significant that puts a smile on my face for the simple fact that sometimes things just go your way. Let me explain.

After my Zumba class a week ago, I was headed home to relax. Thanks to daylight saving time, it now stays lighter later in the evening, which is nice; however, it does pose a challenge in one sense. Normally, before we spring forward, I leave the gym and it is usually dark out as the sun has already set by 7:00 p.m. Now, when I leave, I get to enjoy some sunlight for a short time. Because of this shift, sunny days can prove to be blinding when trying to see your way out of a crowded parking lot.

What put a smile on my face this time was the fact that despite the sun's valiant attempt to keep me from seeing what was ahead, my car, Gandalf, stepped in and very strategically used the part of the car between my front windshield and passenger side window to keep me safe. I thought how fortuitous it was that my car was in the perfect position to provide just the barrier I needed at that exact moment.

Here is yet another example…

Now we've all felt the frustration of trying to figure out how to fold a stupid fitted sheet. I finally mastered that thanks to YouTube. What I have NOT mastered is how to figure out, as I am about to put the freakin' thing on my bed after washing it, which is the short side and which is the long side. I flip that bleepin' thing around and around and STILL get it wrong. I finally managed to get it right on the first try, for ONCE, and I thought how glad I was that I finally mastered that task…well at least until the next time I wash my sheets.

…and the examples continue…

Thanks to of the age of electronics, I am now privy to the joys of the USB cord. I think my stats would show that out of 100 times, I probably insert the end in the correct way on the first try *MAYBE* once. There really is a certain satisfaction to getting it right the first time. As I was syncing up my iPhone the other day, I picked up the USB cord and, with a bit of trepidation, I neared the port and found it went RIGHT IN!! SCORE!!

…and continue still…

Now, this one has only happened once in the 25 years since I started driving. (HOLY CRAP!! 25 YEARS?!?!) Last summer, I had the misfortune of getting my beloved Gandalf backed into in a parking lot. Because of this, I ended up driving a rental car for a week or so. During this time, I got to witness something that made my geekiness *jump* for joy!

While waiting in the left-hand turn lane, I noticed that the blinker of the car in front of me was in PERFECT synchronicity with the blinker on my rental car!! Now, I know that this normally happens, but usually it only lasts a few blinks. Then the ugliness of the alternating lights rears its head, and it's back to business as usual. This was *not* the case this time…believe me…I watched <u>closely</u> to make sure. My heart leapt, as I doubted this would ever again happen, and only did so because I was in a rental car.

I hope you find time to notice and appreciate the little things like these. They may seem childish and insignificant to others, but if they put a smile on your face, they are totally worth it!

I often laugh at the fact that when it comes to my fitted sheet and USB cord, I have a 50/50 chance of getting it right. Why is it that 90% of the time I'm wrong?! That's some crazy math, in my opinion. Here's hoping we all continue to enjoy and appreciate life's little surprises.

Definition, Please

Sitting on my desk at work is a daily calendar that is filled with facts about left-handers. Being a southpaw, I find it very interesting how differently I view the world around me because there are many things we lefties have to adapt to in order to go on with our day-to-day activities. It actually made me giggle one day when a coworker commented how cool it was that I could write something down *and* use the mouse at the same time since I used a different hand for each task. I never really thought much about that, but I guess it can come in handy for sure. Maybe that makes me just a fraction more efficient. (Hey, a girl can dream!) Lately, I've been wondering what else in my life has helped define who I am.

First and foremost, what would I be without a name? From the minute we're born, and in many cases even before we're born, we are defined by our parents and the sum of their experiences. There are many reasons why a certain name is chosen. In my case, I was named Robyn because of a beloved uncle Bob (Robert) on my mom's side of the family.

Now, the choice could have been made to spell my name with an "i" instead of a "y," but the latter was decided upon and here I am. I rarely meet another person with the same spelling I was given, but when it does happen, it is an instant bonding moment. Yes, I'm weird like that. I am also used to spelling my name for people. It's what I've always done. Sadly enough, I am so used to spelling my name for people, that I once did that for none other than my own mother when giving her my email address. I guess it was just a friendly reminder to her in case she forgot how she spelled my name…when she…ummm…*named* me.

As many of my friends know, I am originally from a different state in which I currently live. Now keep in mind, I've been here since I was six years old, but being that I am currently in Texas, I am constantly referred to as a Yankee by those native to these borders. I

108

don't have an accent, so it makes it difficult for people to place where I'm from. I was even told once that I have a "generic newscaster's voice." Uh...thanks? What's funny is when I travel outside of the state and am asked where I'm from (meaning where I currently live), I usually get a response such as, "Oh really?!" It's as if I've given them a bit of trivia or something.

It was funny, several years ago at a wedding up north, I told some family members that it would take me about three hours to get home after I flew back. You see, I had driven to my parents' house so we could all take the same flight out and only have to rent one car. Their jaws dropped at the thought of a drive that, to them, would take them through several states. Those of us in Texas know that a three-hour drive is no big deal and have probably made such a trip a plethora of times.

Now I want you to pretend for a minute that each of us is our own mix of spices. My ingredients would read something like: *Contains left-handed Yankee with a "y" who lives in Texas and missed her calling as a journalist but doesn't mind a road trip.* Come on...who wouldn't buy THAT?!?! I'd probably name my spice something like *Perspectiva de Primavera.* It sounds great but simply means *Robyn's perspective.* (Sidebar - my Spanish teacher used to call me "Primavera," since robins come out in the spring...although that's only the "i" kind of robins, but close enough I guess.)

Now as far as I'm concerned, my P de P spice is the perfect complement for EVERYTHING! Each and every person feels the same way whether they realize it or not. As you could imagine, though, my mix doesn't always go with everyone else's, but after all, when it comes to life, it's all about variety. Here's to us all learning to embrace our "ingredients" and appreciate the subtle and awe-inspiring assortments out there.

I used to joke that my dog, Maggie, was made up of spare parts. Her head looked like a beagle. Her legs were red and white spotted,

109

and her body was black and white spotted with a big black spot on her side. I guess, after thinking about it, we all are made up of spare parts, the difference being that our parts are actually our experiences. It's these experiences that continue to mold and define us and, much like cooking spices, can spill over into other things we touch.

Life is not about making others just like us, as if we're cookie-cutter patterns, but rather it is a way to let others see your perspective. Whether they are open to trying something new is dependent upon them and their sense of openness and adventure.

Balancing the Equation

I am not a fan of math. That being said, I see it the same way I see laundry – a necessary evil. There really is no escaping it. It is vital in everything we do. We can't successfully double a recipe without it. We can't determine without math which is the better buy when comparing toilet paper. Most of us don't have jobs where we spend all day writing complex equations on a whiteboard, but our lives are governed by numbers whether we realize it or not.

Each person is represented by a myriad of numbers that define their lives. From the very beginning we are assigned a birthdate that affects how the world views us and how we view the world. Age is a state of mind, but in reality, it's a number...that's all.

Our height and weight are defined by numbers. There is a stigma that has been put on those numbers that can make someone feel inferior, ashamed, or even ridiculed because they are too far in one direction. Again, these are just numbers.

The funny thing is that they're everywhere, but we've gotten so used to it that we may not realize just how many are used to associate us with the world. You have your phone number, social security number, salary, blood pressure...and the list goes on and on. The bottom line is that these numbers are inanimate objects. They only have power over us because we've given meaning to each of them. Some of us put more emphasis on one over the other...such as our weight or how quickly we can finish a 5K. Even as I'm typing this, my computer is telling me how many words I've written as if something amazing will happen once I reach a certain limit.

There really is no escaping the great numerical overlords, so instead I'm just going to have to live with them the best I can. While some, like my driver's license number, will always be associated with me, there are some that I can choose to give more or less emphasis to moving forward. Emotions seem to appear as the result of a number changing - tears of joy when welcoming a first child into the world, fear from hearing a shocking test result, or concern over how you will be able to afford to pay your bills when you've lost a job and the only income you have is now gone.

There is one truth in math that I do agree with, and that's having a balanced equation. Our plethora of numbers can very easily tip our scale in one direction or the other and instantly cause an imbalance in our lives. Regardless of how far the range can sway, it will usually come back to the middle every so often. I say that it's time we choose what defines us. Sure, the numbers will always be there, but I've realized that what's important can't be defined numerically but rather felt emotionally. Maybe in the end it's the results of the numbers that drive our happiness, and I should be glad they're behind the scenes shaping my life and making me the person I am today and am yet to be.

I'm finding that I'm letting numbers rule me less than I used to in the past. This really is huge for me, as I've always lived my life by them. I'm not saying I've gone off the deep end by throwing caution to the wind. I'm too level-headed for that. I just mean that I know there will always be someone taller or shorter, richer or poorer, smarter or more talented. The difference is now, I'm not comparing myself to them. I'm trying to be the best me I can be, and I'm letting the numbers take care of themselves.

Revealing My Inner Geek

I will admit that I am a geek and a nerd at heart. It's not something I'm ashamed of, but rather quite proud of because I believe that geeks and nerds are always learning and appreciate things on a completely different level than most. While some people spend their time watching reality *TV*, I try to surround myself with plain old reality. I listen to podcasts about space and science. I watch shows about how the mind works and what new discoveries have been documented. I get the biggest kick out of learning something new each day.

What really fascinates me is when I can be watching a show or listening to a new or never-before-heard episode of one of my podcasts and something is said that completely blows my mind. When that happens, it usually gets my brain going in a thousand directions and causes me to rethink that which I previously believed to be fact. What I love even more is that every time scientists think they've figured something out, the universe sends them a big piece of humble pie and proceeds to show them what they never imagined possible.

It is said that no object can go as fast as the speed of light, but rather it can only *approach* the speed of light, as time slows down the closer you get to the target. Having stated that, there is one thing that *can* travel faster than the speed of light, and that is the expansion of the universe. It would have to be able to do so. If that is the case, then at what speed is the expansion traveling? Infinity speed? Into what is it expanding? Maybe we just *think* it's expanding when in fact there is something else going on out there.

Finally, I would like to propose a question to you which I also posed to a very well-known astrophysicist. Dark matter has fascinated me for quite some time. I think it's because no one knows what it is and it appears to be everywhere. Here was my question – If at some time in the future we discover what dark matter is, and we are able to control it, *and* it is dark matter that separates us from the Andromeda galaxy, would we then be able to prevent the Andromeda and Milky

Way galaxies from colliding? Maybe my last question shouldn't be *would* we, but rather *should* we. Who knows what celestial surprises we would have in store?

Welcome to my brain, where geeks and nerds rule the world!

I often wonder if others think about these things. Do they find this kind of conversation as thought-provoking as I do? Intelligence is such an attractive quality that I feel is dwindling the more technology is becoming a part of our lives. We don't seek out the truth but rather believe what is told to us. Critical thinking is quickly becoming a lost art. We have so much information at our fingertips, yet many don't know how to properly and politely carry on a conversation that has any depth to it.

I think that is why I enjoy science. They are never so arrogant as to think that their conclusions are absolutely correct. They concede that there is a possibility that they could have all their work proven wrong when new information comes to light. Sure, you can have pride in your work, but a sign of true intelligence comes from the realization that you could be wrong.

For example, Ptolemy believed that the Earth was the center of the universe and explained the retrograde motion of the other planets and sun through the use of Epicycles. This meant that not only did they revolve around the Earth, but they also followed a circular orbit of their own. It wasn't until Copernicus, 13 centuries later (WOW!), made the suggestion that the sun, not the Earth, was the center of the universe. We now know that it is the sun that is center of our solar system and not the universe as it was previously believed.

Think though, about how many people believed these earlier facts to be true just because. We should always question the things around us. After all, you may have an idea that, to you, is very obvious but to others had never crossed their minds.

Reflecting Thoughts

In recent days, I've spoken with friends and several times the phrase, "Hindsight's always 20/20," has come up. It really is interesting when you gain perspective after some time has passed that you can finally see things clearly. We often find ourselves reflecting on what has happened to us only to realize how much we've changed or learned. Today, while on my way to work, I had one of those moments, and what was reflected back made my heart smile.

I've looked to the past before for answers, and today what was reflected back was a beautiful sunrise. Of course, I think about the future, and am rather excited by what it holds, but excitement in my case is not anxiety. My past no longer makes me depressed, but rather who I am today. Someone recently said that their past was the best worst thing that's happened to them, and I could totally identify with that description.

As for me, I couldn't think of a better image to represent my life right now than an incredible sunrise. How perfectly that reflected my present, and what a peaceful present it is.

You always have the choice to direct your focus wherever you want. Acknowledging where you've come from is healthy. What many people often forget is just how far they've come. It's as if they can't see the forest for the trees. Use your past as a guide or a living rule book of what to and not to do. Just remember not to keep your focus there or you'll miss all the amazing things in front of you.

My sister recently told me a story that I wanted to share, as it perfectly described yesterday morning for me.

The story is about a little boy with cancer who had a nice man who drove him to and from his chemo treatments each time. He would drive up to the little boy's house and watch as he'd skip out the front door down to the car and climb in with a big grin on his face. Each time on the way home the little boy would be horrifically sick and appeared to be the complete opposite of the spirited child who greeted him earlier that day. This went on for several treatments. The boy would happily skip out the door wearing a huge grin and arrive home, sometimes being carried to the door due to the lack of strength to walk.

Finally, one day on the way to his treatment, the nice man asked the little boy how he could be so happy each time he saw him, knowing where he was being taken and knowing that he'd end up so sick on the way home. The little boy looked at the nice man and told him that he was happy because going to his treatments didn't automatically mean he was going to end up sick. He said he didn't worry about what *might* happen, as it was a waste of energy. He explained that if he came out feeling upset and had his treatment and didn't get sick afterwards, then he suffered once for nothing. If he came out feeling upset and ended up sick afterwards, then he suffered twice. But, if he came out feeling happy and didn't get sick, then he didn't suffer at all. *That* is why he skipped out of the house. He was always happy because *today* might finally be the day that he could enjoy his ride home and skip back up to his house with a smile on his face.

Now, my sister would agree with me that our mom has a PhD in worrying. She can worry for things that may happen, things that did happen, things that maybe – if the conditions were *just* right – might happen. She suffers unnecessarily so often, but we'd probably say that, for her, it's just a conditioned response. Thanks to my sister, though, I will keep this story in my head whenever my first reaction is to worry unnecessarily.

I have shared this story many times with many people. I've found it is so universal, as it seems it is our nature to think the worst in most situations. Hope is an amazing thing. So often we lose sight of that. Learning to take a step back and not be immediately reactive to a potential situation can make all the difference. What I find even more profound with this story is that lessons can be taught from even the youngest of people. The question really is, are you open to receiving that lesson when it is presented to you?

The Boxing Ring

I'm feeling like a boxer right now. That's the only way I can describe my dating life. I started off almost two years ago with the ding of the first bell following my divorce.

Round 1

I take hit after hit while trying to duck a weave to avoid the next impending blow. Every once in a while, I land a good upper cut or left hook (yes, I'm a lefty). After being completely spent, I hear the bell ring. FINALLY, I can go to my corner for a rest. A round of unsuccessful dating has completed.

Round 2

I'm slowly learning to read my opponent (the dating pool). I'm able to evade a hit or two since there seems to be a pattern. Just when I'm feeling confident, my opponent throws in a fake right followed by a left. I did NOT see that one coming. My head is spinning as I don't know what just hit me. I feel my knees go weak, and just as I'm about to give up for good, I hear the bell.

Round 3

My legs are wobbly, yet I somehow gather the strength to stand. I decide to change my strategy, so this time I come out punching. I don't give my opponent time to react. I'm taking charge. Things are looking up as the round is finally going my way. I can see round after round of this and am so pumped that it's finally working. Just then my target begins dodging my advancing shots. It's obvious this round isn't going anywhere. DING DING!...whatever!

Round 4

As I step up to the sound of the bell, my strategy is to just look busy for this round. I don't want to actually throw any punches, but rather just keep moving. This works for a while and then time's up, so I head to my corner.

Round...oh, enter whatever number you want...I think I'm approaching infinity at this point.

I basically took a break the last round and gained a little strength. I'm feeling my confidence coming back, so I decide to throw my hat in the ring yet again. Maybe it's a false sense of hope this time, but even Rocky had his moments. This time my plan is to take this round with caution. Yes, I'm cautiously hopeful. I'm sure it's going to leave me bruised and beaten, and I'm afraid I'm going to get hurt, but it beats sitting in the corner.

I have to say that this still makes me laugh. Dating is hard. Anyone who tells you differently is either lying or knows some sort of secret that they're not sharing with the rest of us. What is important regardless of what you go through is to make sure that you keep your sense of humor about you. Putting yourself out there time and time again is exhausting both physically and emotionally, but being able to laugh in the face of all of it is very powerful.

I remember back when I sold Tupperware that they told us a story about a lady just starting out. In her training, she was told that for every nine no's she'd get, she would get one yes. This stuck with her. She decided to go door-to-door around a neighborhood, as this was how things were done early on. She went from one house to the next, each time receiving negative reactions to what she was offering. Finally at her 9th house, she presented her products to the homeowner and got turned down. When she heard him tell her "no," she responded with an enthusiastic, "Thanks!" and bounded down the stairs with a definite pep in her step.

Her potential customer found her reaction very odd, so he asked her why she was so happy when he had just turned her down. She explained in her training that for every nine no's she would get one yes. To her, that HAD to mean that the next house was a yes! The homeowner was so amused that he decided to purchase some of her products, and the rest, for her, is history.

I often think of this when meeting someone new on a date. I guess the optimist in me hopes that even if that date doesn't work out that I'm able to make it until the bell rings and the 10th round ends with a knockout relationship!

It Takes a Village

Life can be a big complicated mess. There is no rulebook and there are no instructions that tell you how to avoid getting hurt or making a mistake 100% of the time. We all live by trial and error. You could say that we all just make things up as we go along. We have no way to know what the future will hold, but many of our decisions are based on what has happened to us in the past. How then do we make it through each day without either feeling defeated or scared? We do so with a little help from our friends.

Think about the close relationships you've had over the years. These can range from friendships to marriages and everything in between. How many of them have you asked advice about? I think, for me, it would be safe to say that at one point or another I've asked advice about each and every one of them. This means that not only am I the sum of my experiences, but I'm the sum of the advice I've received. I have learned that my perspective isn't always the clearest in each situation, so speaking with someone objective makes a world of difference.

I'm very grateful for those friends and family who are always there to lend an ear as well as some words of wisdom. I also am thankful to those with whom I share a relationship for seeking out advice from those they confide in when needed. What still amazes me is when I get just the right call or text from just the right person at just the right time. I believe that angels come in all shapes and forms, and I'd have to say that's probably my favorite.

None of us is perfect, which means that no relationship is, either. It takes work from both partners, whether it be platonic or romantic. So many people are closed off to communication and would rather internalize what happens to them. I have definitely learned that it is best to not waste my time trying to explain who I am to someone who is committed to misunderstanding me. Many times, those from who I seek counsel, simply confirm what I was already thinking.

121

Additionally, they have kept me sane, kept me honest, and kept me accountable. The best thing about this kind of interaction is that you can always pay it forward, and that's what I intend to keep doing.

Nothing gives me a bigger thrill than learning something new. As I've mentioned before, I was lovingly referred to as "The Mouth of Unwanted Knowledge" in high school, so as you can imagine, new tidbits of trivia are always music to my ears. I guess I enjoy learning when it's on my terms. This means I don't have an assignment or homework to do and can watch or read things that pique *my* interests.

I can usually be found watching shows on the Discovery, History, and National Geographic channels, as I find them completely intriguing as well as educational. I enjoy listening to podcasts from Radiolab, as they cover a myriad of topics and always put an interesting twist on what it is that they are discussing. What I have found more recently, is that in addition to learning new information about other things, I find it even more interesting when I learn something new about myself.

Someone once asked me, "In what five-year period do you think you grew the most intellectually and emotionally?" In years past, my answer without question would have included the ages 18-23. After all, during this time I moved away and started college, got married, graduated from college, bought and sold our first house, bought our second house and was in the beginnings of our struggle with infertility. I'd have to say that after seeing those in type, they are some pretty heavy issues to deal with. Of course, those are just the tip of the iceberg, but you get the idea. So while those issues have definitely helped to shape me into the person I am today, my journey is by no means over, which means I never stop learning.

Someday I'd really like to learn something the easy way. I've had many conversations with G-d where I say that I really will appreciate and remember the lesson if it can just be a *little* bit easier. Why is it then that G-d insists that I learn everything the hard way? Is it just funnier to watch how I can find new and better ways to royally screw up my life or whatever situation I'm in at the time?

I can honestly say that my mind feels like a sponge most of the time. This is very two-sided, though. Sure, I can soak up information I find interesting, but like a sponge, there are many cases when I'd like to wring it out so I can rid it of a bad thought, decision, or embarrassing moment. Needless to say, more than anything, it is my mind that gets in my way. It isn't until I'm able to "wring it out," so to say, that I can finally get some clarity. I can be having a good day and all it takes is a single random negative thought to pop into my head to instantly change my mood. It really is amazing just how much power your brain has over your actions. After all, whether you think you can or think you can't, you're right.

This week I proved to myself that it's my brain and not my body holding me back…and probably always has. Let me share yet another recent discovery. Each time I go to the gym for a workout, I always finish it by completing a 5K. I say completing it because I don't *always* run the entire way. As I was coming to the last lap on this particular day, I began wondering if I could run a little faster. My pace is usually at a comfortable 5.5 mph, which is way faster than I ever thought I'd be able to run when I started exercising. I began increasing the speed until I realized I was running at 9 mph!!

If you had asked me earlier that day if I could run that fast, I would have said no way! Did I fall? No! Did I die? Wouldn't be writing this if I had! Did I feel like I had overcome something that had been holding me back? You bet your sweet bippies!

What I've discovered now, is that once I learn to find a way to turn off the negative thoughts in this crazy brain of mine, there will be no stopping me. I may still have many difficult and challenging lessons to learn, but that's not the point. The point, my friends, is that I found that my only limits are the ones *I* set. Even more important is that I learned something new about myself; I continue to learn new things about myself, and most importantly, I will *never* stop learning!! I challenge you to do the same!

Some lessons stay with you and some you have to face again and again. What makes one easier than the other? What makes it stick? For me, I believe it to be awareness. This can't just be until it becomes second nature, but always. I am guilty about just going through the motions when it comes to aspects of my life. At times, this is just temporary and then something snaps me out of my trance and I'm back on track. Sometimes though, it takes someone or something more profound to bring me to this conclusion. My goal then has to be to raise my level of awareness and always strive to better myself. I just know that if I can do it, anyone can!

CPSIA information can be obtained
at www.ICGtesting.com
Printed in the USA
LVHW03s1556180818
587376LV00001B/71/P